amazing grace

by
Michael Cristofer

SAMUEL FRENCH, INC.
45 WEST 25TH STREET   **NEW YORK 10010**
7623 SUNSET BOULEVARD   **HOLLYWOOD 90046**
LONDON   *TORONTO*

IMPORTANT BILLING AND CREDIT REQUIREMENTS

All producers of AMAZING GRACE *must* give credit to the Author of the Play in all programs distributed in connection with performances of the Play and in all instances in which the title of the Play appears for purposes of advertising, publicizing or otherwise exploiting the Play and/or a production. The name of the Author *must* also appear on a separate line, on which no other name appears, immediately following the title, and *must* appear in size of type not less than fifty percent the size of the title type.

Also, in all programs for the Play, Producers are required to include the following:

> The Pittsburg Public Theatre (Edward Gilbert, Artistic
> Director) presented the world premiere of AMAZING
> GRACE in October 1995 under the direction of Edward Gilbert

In all first and second class stage productions on the title page of the Playbill or equivalent house program in which full production credits are given, the following shall be included in no less than 20% the size of the title:

> Produced in New York by Blue Light Theatre Company

In addition, the following must appear in all programs distributed in connection with productions of the Play:

> "PLEASE HELP ME I'M FALLING"
> (Hal Blair, Don Robertson) © 1960 CHAPPELL & CO. (ASCAP)
> & DON ROBERTSON MUSIC CORP. (UKNOWN)
> ALL RIGHTS RESERVED. USED BY PERMISSION

THEATRE FOUR
ROGER ALAN GINDI, General Manager

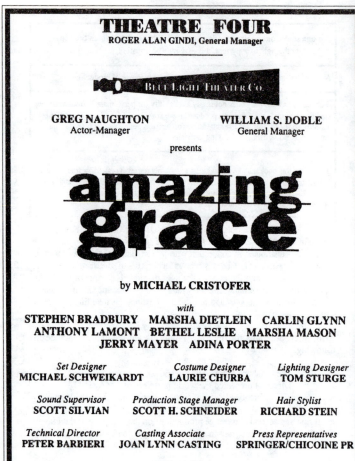

BLUE LIGHT THEATER CO.

GREG NAUGHTON
Actor-Manager

WILLIAM S. DOBLE
General Manager

presents

amazing grace

by MICHAEL CRISTOFER

with

**STEPHEN BRADBURY   MARSHA DIETLEIN   CARLIN GLYNN
ANTHONY LAMONT   BETHEL LESLIE   MARSHA MASON
JERRY MAYER   ADINA PORTER**

Set Designer
MICHAEL SCHWEIKARDT

Costume Designer
LAURIE CHURBA

Lighting Designer
TOM STURGE

Sound Supervisor
SCOTT SILVIAN

Production Stage Manager
SCOTT H. SCHNEIDER

Hair Stylist
RICHARD STEIN

Technical Director
PETER BARBIERI

Casting Associate
JOAN LYNN CASTING

Press Representatives
SPRINGER/CHICOINE PR

Directed by
EDWARD GILBERT

Blue Light Theater Company gratefully acknowledges
RICHARD W. SORENSON AMERICAN INTERACTIVE MEDIA NEWMAN'S OWN
for their support of this production

Pittsburgh Public Theater (Edward Gilbert, Artistic Director) presented the world premiere of *Amazing Grace* in October 1995 under the direction of Edward Gilbert.

http://www.bluelight.org

for

MARSHA MASON
and
EDWARD GILBERT

ACT I

*(Lights up on SELENA GOODALL—She sits doing needle-
point. She is dressed in pink pajamas. She is beatifically
calm and quite happy.*
*Lights up on the "WITNESSES" who play all the various char-
acters.*
Please note that this play should be performed on a bare stage.)

SELENA. *(Looking at needlepoint.)* Well, this is going to
be very nice. You can tell, you know? You can tell right away.
Soon as you start. From the first stitch. See it start, see it end.
(She smiles and sings.) 'I once was blind but now I see.'

WITNESS. How are you feeling now?

SELENA. Fine. Nervous. I suppose that's natural.

WITNESS. Can I get you anything? Glass of water, cup of
coffee?

WITNESS. Can you tell us how many?

WITNESS. Can you tell us why?

WITNESS. Do you remember?

SELENA. *(Counting stitches.)* ... five, six, seven.

WITNESS. Do you want to tell me what happened?

WITNESS. Do you still have this heat in your hands?

WITNESS. Do you still have this power?

SELENA. *(Looking at needlepoint.)* I wish I could finish
this. It's going to be so pretty.

7

WITNESS. You ain't thinking straight. Are you?

WITNESS. Is it true what she said? Are you flirting with me?

WITNESS. Do you still live in your mother's house?

(Lights change. One WITNESS—an older woman—gets into a wheelchair. Another WITNESS wheels her down to a table. SELENA goes to the table and starts feeding the woman.)

SELENA. ... and the man gets out of his car and goes up to the farmer. Is this right? Wait just a minute. Yes. He gets out of his car and goes up to the farmer and he says, I just had to stop and speak to you because I have never seen a pig like that before. I have never seen a pig with a wooden leg. *(SELENA continues feeding her mother. The mother—ESTHER GOODALL—seems to be a stroke victim. She doesn't speak or respond.)* Well, says the farmer, that is no ordinary pig. See, about a year ago, we had a fire in the house. Dead of night, everybody asleep. Well, that pig ran into the house, ran smack up the stairs, into my bedroom, woke me up, woke up my wife—he was near dead—you have to exaggerate this part—led us through the smoke and the flames and saved us, hallelujah. And when he got us outside, that pig turned around and ran right back inside, into the flames and the ... uh ... what else? ... the falling timbers and the sparks and he saved our two children, too. Brought them right outside, glory, glory ... *(She leans close to her mother.)* Are you following this story? I know I don't tell it very well ... *(ESTHER suddenly smacks SELENA on the cheek—not hard, but SELENA is stunned. Then she continues.)*

So the man says, golly, that's one heck of a story. But it still doesn't explain why that same pig has a wooden leg. Well, said the farmer, you have to understand, a pig like that, you don't eat it all at once. *(SELENA laughs.)* Well, I died when I heard that. It was so terrible, it was such a terrible joke, but I couldn't help it. *(She looks at her mother.)* Do you think that's funny? I bet you do. *(SELENA takes two pills from a bottle and puts them into ESTHER's mouth, massaging her throat to help her swallow.)* Are you laughing in there? Are you? Huh? Are you laughing?

(No response. SELENA takes some pills and swallows them herself. Lights change. A WITNESS plays the DRUGGIST.)

DRUGGIST. Are you Mrs. Goodall?

SELENA. No, That's my mother. They're for my mother. Esther Goodall.

DRUGGIST. Well, we did not fill this prescription originally...

SELENA. No. I know that.

DRUGGIST. ... and I can't make out the date here on this label ...

SELENA. I just need to have it renewed.

DRUGGIST. I understand that ...

SELENA. She needs it badly.

DRUGGIST. She must be in a lot of pain.

SELENA. Yes. She is.

DRUGGIST. These are very strong.

SELENA. Please.

DRUGGIST. Well ...

SELENA. Thank you. I do appreciate it. And do you carry shoelaces?

(Lights change. A WITNESS picks up a bag of groceries and comes to SELENA.)

VIVIAN. ... and I said, well give them to me, I'll bring them over right now.

SELENA. Oh, what are you doing? I can manage ...

VIVIAN. Never mind.

SELENA. I can manage my own groceries.

VIVIAN. Not if you ain't feeling right. *(To ESTHER's face.)* Hello, Esther, how you keeping?

(ESTHER does not respond.)

SELENA. Oh, there ain't nothing wrong with me. I just can't seem to get out of these pajamas today.

VIVIAN. Well, that old fool Hawkins made it sound like you were peeing green or something. And would I take these things by ...

SELENA. I just order by phone so I don't have to spend so much time in there ...

VIVIAN. I said sure I would ...

SELENA. The way he looks at me ...

VIVIAN. Oh, he looks at his own mother that way. At his age. He can't have but a half inch of pecker left in those drawers.

SELENA. *(Laughs.)* I didn't mean that.

VIVIAN. And what he thinks he can do with that is beyond me.

SELENA. No, It's just I owe him so much money.

VIVIAN. Oh. Oh. Oh. I see.

SELENA. I don't like going in there. That's all.

VIVIAN. Well, a single girl has to be careful—especially if you owe the man money.

SELENA. I don't think ...

VIVIAN. Especially if the man is Marvin Hawkins and his withering weenie.

SELENA. Vivian, oh, how you talk.

VIVIAN. At this age, honey, talk is my only form of self-abuse. *(To ESTHER.)* Excuse me, Esther. *(To SELENA.)* She don't know what I'm saying, does she?

SELENA. I don't know. I don't think so. I hope not.

VIVIAN. *(Pulling tins from grocery bag.)* What's this? You don't have a cat, Selena. Do you?

SELENA. No, of course, I don't ...

VIVIAN. Then what's he sending you cat food for? That fool son of a dingbat.

SELENA. No. I ordered it. There's a stray been coming around.

VIVIAN. Oh.

SELENA. Last few weeks.

VIVIAN. Well, you don't need to go feeding strays when there's barely food for yourself.

SELENA. Well ...

VIVIAN. God, Selena, this is the most peculiar collection of groceries—one roll of toilet paper, a half pint milk, a bag of Cheese Doodles and a Baby Ruth. And what in God's name ...

SELENA. Rats.

VIVIAN. What?

SELENA. There's rats in the cellar. I been spreading this poison down there.

VIVIAN. Oh my, I can stand just about anything—but rats in the cellar, that must be my limit. Why don't you get that stray cat down there.

SELENA. Well, that's an idea, isn't it?

VIVIAN. Yes, it is and it reminds me—ain't it peculiar how the mind works? —But did you see? They got a fortune-teller at the Holiday Inn now?

SELENA. They have what?

VIVIAN. At the Holiday Inn, they have a fortune-teller.

SELENA. They do not.

VIVIAN. In the bar. In the bar of the Holiday Inn. She's there, honey. She goes from table to table and she tells fortunes.

SELENA. They never.

VIVIAN. She tells the future for you while you suck on your whiskey. *(SELENA laughs.)* Well, it's not funny.

(SELENA and VIVIAN laugh.)

SELENA. Well, it is. Where did you hear this?

VIVIAN. It was in the newspaper. She won't say anything bad that she sees. Just the good things. And the worst is, she says it's a gift. She says it's the Lord speaking through her.

SELENA. That's blasphemy, isn't it?

VIVIAN. And she just looks deep into the eyes of who she's seeing and she disappears. Well, she don't disappear cause you can still see her, but what happens is she spouts out the future or whatever else she sees, the words just leap-frog right out of her mouth and she has no control of it, like she isn't even there.

SELENA. You think that's the truth?

VIVIAN. I don't know. But I've a mind to go down there and see.

SELENA. You wouldn't do that.

VIVIAN. I might. If I thought I had a future worth looking at.

SELENA. Yes ...

(SELENA fiddles with ESTHER's hair.)

VIVIAN. How's Esther doing these days?

SELENA. Oh, she's alright, I guess. I don't know. Same as ever. I put her in front of the T.V. She watches the bible station. She seems to enjoy that.

VIVIAN. She'll outlive us all.

SELENA. They're cutting back the programs again. I don't get the checks the way I used to. I was thinking, honest to God, I'm going to have to find some work.

VIVIAN. *(Laughs.)* Doing what?!

SELENA. Well ...

VIVIAN. What would you ever do?

SELENA. Well, I can sew. I can clean.

VIVIAN. *(Laughs.)* For money?

SELENA. It's a thought.

VIVIAN. I didn't know it was that bad.

SELENA. Well, it isn't.

(SELENA turns on the television. The WITNESSES speak the

words coming from the bible station.)

WITNESSES. 'And when I kept silent, my bones grew old through my groaning all the day long.'

VIVIAN. There's always a way to carry on, Selena. You'll find it. You're one of God's own saints, honey. He'll show you the way.

(VIVIAN goes.)

WITNESSES. 'For day and night your hand was heavy upon me, my vitality was turned into the drought of summer.

'I acknowledged my sin to you, and my iniquity I have not hidden.

'I said, "I will confess my transgressions to the lord" and you forgave the iniquity of my sin.'

(During the above, SELENA goes to the table, opens a can of cat food, sits at the table and, as she watches the T.V., she eats the cat food. One of the WITNESSES comes down to the table to play the FORTUNE-TELLER. SELENA wheels her mother upstage and then exits. Two more WITNESSES— a man and a woman—come down. They are a couple seeking help from the FORTUNE-TELLER. Sounds of a bar are in the background.
The FORTUNE-TELLER is an ordinary woman. She looks like a housewife, not a gypsy. As the words from the bible station end, she speaks immediately.)

FORTUNE-TELLER. I live right near there.
WIFE. You do?
WITNESSES. You are my hiding place.
FORTUNE-TELLER. Right near Millerton. On the county road.
WIFE. We're neighbors.
MAN. Yes. I guess we are.

WIFE. I bet I pass your house once a day. Well.

WITNESSES. You shall preserve me from trouble.

FORTUNE-TELLER. Would you like me to walk with you a little?

WITNESSES. I will instruct you and teach you in the way you should go.

MAN. My wife has a question.

FORTUNE-TELLER. Well, I don't know that I can answer a question.

WITNESSES. I will guide you with my eye.

(The remaining WITNESSES exit.)

FORTUNE-TELLER. But I think I can walk with you and talk a little bit.

MAN. What about?

FORTUNE-TELLER. Oh, I don't know. You have to say what it's about. Sometimes it's the future and sometimes it's the past. And I'll be clear with you, sometimes it's not about anything worth listening to, but it don't do any harm and it won't cost you anything and that's all I can promise you.

MAN. Alright then.

WIFE. Yes.

FORTUNE-TELLER. Let me see now ... Let me see. I could walk with you right from this table, through that door to the parking lot, all the way across the parking lot and I could get into the Plymouth with you and sit in the back seat next to the ... next to that ... what *is* that in the back seat taking up all that room?

WIFE. That's my sewing machine. I was bringing it to my sister ...

FORTUNE-TELLER. ... and drive and drive and nobody's talking except in whispers, 'she's still asleep,' 'well, try not to wake her until we get home,' and stopping the car under the carport and 'hold the door while I get out' and trying not to trip up on the bricks on the walk where the good grass is on the right and the left side just never got the sun.

MAN. Well, that's true, isn't it? The whole left side of the lawn just never, ever ...

WIFE. Shh ...

FORTUNE-TELLER. And through the front door, carefully, what am I carrying? I have to be so careful, you get the light, I'm going straight upstairs ...

WIFE. What are you carrying?

FORTUNE-TELLER. I can manage.

WIFE. Do you know what it is?

FORTUNE-TELLER. Just down the hall to the second door...

WIFE. Is it a baby? Is that a baby you see?

(During the above, SELENA enters, watching the FORTUNE-TELLER.)

FORTUNE-TELLER. ... and open it and oh ...

WIFE. We're praying for me to be pregnant.

FORTUNE-TELLER. ... it has a smell ... it has a smell of ... no, this is not the right room. This is not where I was going.

MAN. Where *are* you going?

WIFE. We're praying for a baby ...

(The FORTUNE-TELLER stands up suddenly and faces SELENA. At the same moment, ESTHER stands up from her wheelchair.)

FORTUNE-TELLER. This is the sick room. This ...

MAN. No. We don't have a sick room.

WIFE. No.

FORTUNE-TELLER. This is the old lady's room.

WIFE. Old lady?

MAN. We don't have an old lady.

WIFE. No.

MAN. This is not about us.

WIFE. *(To FORTUNE-TELLER.)* Where are you now?
MAN. Let it go ...
WIFE. No.
FORTUNE-TELLER. Where am I now?
WIFE. Yes. Where?
MAN. Let it go. This is not us.
WIFE. No.
FORTUNE-TELLER. This is not you.
WOMAN. We were praying ...
MAN. Let it go. This is not us.

(WOMAN buries her head in her husband's shoulder.)

FORTUNE-TELLER. This is the old lady's room.

(ESTHER moves toward us. She is younger now and when she speaks, she speaks from the past. As the MAN and WOMAN exit ...)

ESTHER. This is my room.
WIFE. No. This is not us. No.
ESTHER. I was here. I was in my room.
FORTUNE-TELLER. The old lady was in her room. But she wasn't old then.
ESTHER. I could hear ...
FORTUNE-TELLER. She could hear ...
ESTHER. I could hear the sound.
FORTUNE-TELLER. ... the sound. What is that?
ESTHER. What is it?

(During this, SELENA moves to the FORTUNE-TELLER.)

FORTUNE-TELLER. *(To SELENA.)* Is it you?
SELENA. I don't know.
FORTUNE-TELLER. Do I know you?
SELENA. No I just ...

FORTUNE-TELLER. Is it you I hear?

SELENA. I don't know.

ESTHER. I could hear it.

FORTUNE-TELLER. Who is it?

ESTHER. I could hear the sound.

FORTUNE-TELLER. Where is it coming from?

SELENA. I don't know. I can't say. I just wanted to speak to you.

FORTUNE-TELLER. Listen. Do you hear?

SELENA. Do I hear?

FORTUNE-TELLER. No. Listen.

ESTHER. I could hear it.

FORTUNE-TELLER. Leaving the room and moving now, quietly, where are we going? Do you know?

ESTHER. Downstairs.

FORTUNE-TELLER. Down the stairs.

SELENA. Yes.

FORTUNE-TELLER. Do you follow me? Do you know what I'm saying?

SELENA. I think I do.

(SELENA sits in a chair. The FORTUNE-TELLER stands behind her.)

FORTUNE-TELLER. To the kitchen. And where is that girl?

SELENA. I was doing the dishes.

FORTUNE-TELLER. She's supposed to be doing these dishes.

SELENA. I was doing the washing up and he'd come up behind me ...

FORTUNE-TELLER/ESTHER. Where is that girl?

SELENA. That's alright. Don't you worry about those dishes. You come with me.

FORTUNE-TELLER. Down the stairs again. It's much cooler now.

SELENA. You be quiet.

ESTHER. I could hear.

SELENA. You do what I say.

FORTUNE-TELLER. Trying to listen and trying not to hear.

ESTHER. I could hear them.

SELENA. You be a good girl.

FORTUNE-TELLER. Yes. You do what Daddy says ...

SELENA. You ain't my daddy.

FORTUNE-TELLER. As good as.

SELENA. You're my stepdaddy.

FORTUNE-TELLER. As good as your daddy.

ESTHER. I could hear them.

FORTUNE-TELLER/ESTHER. *(Together.)* Trying not to make a sound, on the stairs, down to the basement, somebody needs to clean down here, sooner or later, before the dust and the dirt and the ... ohh!

(The FORTUNE-TELLER clasps a hand over SELENA's mouth.)

FORTUNE-TELLER.	ESTHER.
I can see her there.	I saw her there.
I can see her, watching me	I saw her, under
struggle, moving, and he's	the shoulder of his
telling me be still, be	shirt, just her hair
still, little pus, little	at first and a hand
pus, 'fore I break you in	and then his back
half and oh, oh, oh,	rose in front of me
coming up over me like a	like a whale, slow
whale, slow and definite,	and definite, up and
up and down, and there is	down, covering over
no light down here, but	her, so small, she's
my brain was telling me	only eleven I said
even without the light	in my brain and in
I can see this is not	the dark even without
right.	the light, I can see this
	was not right.

ESTHER. I saw her.

FORTUNE-TELLER. She saw me.

ESTHER. Underneath him.

FORTUNE-TELLER. He had his hand ...

ESTHER. ... over her mouth.

FORTUNE-TELLER. ... over my mouth.

FORTUNE-TELLER/ESTHER. She (I) was looking right into my (her) eyes.

FORTUNE-TELLER. My eyes screaming at her, make him stop.

ESTHER. Her eyes looking right at me.

FORTUNE-TELLER. Make him stop this.

ESTHER. Her legs kicking, her arms beating at his back where his shirt was up and his pants pushed down.

FORTUNE-TELLER. Make him stop.

ESTHER. I know what you're doing.

FORTUNE-TELLER. But she stands there in the doorway and she never says a word.

ESTHER. I see what you're doing.

FORTUNE-TELLER. And he keeps on, he keeps on.

FORTUNE-TELLER/ESTHER. I see it.

FORTUNE-TELLER. Make him stop, Mama. Make him stop.

FORTUNE-TELLER/ESTHER. You brought this on yourself.

FORTUNE-TELLER. No.

ESTHER. You brought this sin on yourself.

FORTUNE-TELLER/ESTHER. I have to shut my eyes.

FORTUNE-TELLER. No.

FORTUNE-TELLER/ESTHER. I have to turn away from evil.

FORTUNE-TELLER. And she turns away from me.

FORTUNE-TELLER/ESTHER. I turn away.

FORTUNE-TELLER. She turns away and leaves me.

FORTUNE-TELLER/ESTHER. I turn away.

FORTUNE-TELLER. And he keeps on, he keeps on, he

keeps on ... *(Pause. ESTHER goes back to her wheelchair. The FORTUNE-TELLER takes her hand away from SELENA's mouth. SELENA's mouth is bleeding.)* I'm sorry. Forgive me. I don't know ...

SELENA. It's alright.

FORTUNE-TELLER. This isn't right. Your mouth is bleeding.

(SELENA touches the blood with her finger.)

SELENA. There was no blood then. There never has been. They said I would. Every month. Every woman does. But I never did.

FORTUNE-TELLER. Never?

SELENA. To this day—never. Excuse me. I have to go.

FORTUNE-TELLER. Yes. Go to God. Go to God.

(SELENA goes to wheelchair and brings ESTHER to the table. FORTUNE-TELLER exits. SELENA and ESTHER are alone on stage. SELENA starts to feed ESTHER. ESTHER makes a moaning sound.)

SELENA. Yes, Esther. What is it? Hmmm.

ESTHER. *(Barely audible.)* Ssssowe ...

SELENA. No. Say it again.

ESTHER. *(Barely audible whisper.)* Salt ...

SELENA. Salt. You want some salt. *(She tries the shaker. It's empty.)* Well, there isn't any.

ESTHER. *(Whispered.)* Salt.

SELENA. Here. There's a little pepper left. But there's no salt.

(She puts pepper on ESTHER's food.)

ESTHER. Salt.

SELENA. We have no salt. Do you understand that? We

have no salt because we have no money to buy salt. We have no salt, we have no sugar, we have no flour, no butter, no paper towels, no tea, no eggs, no bread ...

ESTHER. Salt.

SELENA. No! We don't have any! *No salt.* We have half a pint of milk, that's all we have. We have cat food which I have been eating for the last three months, we have a small bag of Cheese Doodles, two tablespoons of coffee, and a candy bar. You see? Here it is. *This is all we have! (Showing the groceries to ESTHER.)* And a single roll of toilet paper. And some dinner for the rats in the cellar.

ESTHER. Salt. *(SELENA starts to shake and cry in despair. She picks up the food and tries to feed it to ESTHER. ESTHER resists. Continues, still a tense whisper.)* Salt.

(SELENA opens the container of rat poison and sprinkles the white powder on ESTHER's food.)

SELENA. There. There's some salt. Alright? There's some salt for you. Are you satisfied now? This is salt. Alright? Hmn? Are you going to eat now? Hmn? Are you? *(She feeds the poisoned food to ESTHER. ESTHER eats it.)* That's better. *(She turns on the television and then continues feeding ESTHER the poison. The WITNESSES return to the stage.)* Oh, look. This is an old, old program. From way back. You remember this program. It's called "Name That Tune". They show these old programs now from twenty, thirty years ago. You remember? You have to run up there and press the buzzer first and then you get to guess the name of the song. *(She hums a song.)* Da-da-da-da-dee-da. Do you know that one? I know that one. Oh, *she* knows it. There she goes Buzz. Buzz. And the name of the song is—"Please Help Me, I'm Falling". She got it. Look at her. She's jumping up and down. She's so happy. Oh my God. Oh my God! She fell. Look at that Esther. She really fell down. *(She sings.)* 'Please help me, I'm falling... '

(SELENA continues feeding her mother the poisoned food.)

WITNESS. And then what did you do?

SELENA. I cleaned up. I did the dishes. I was going to put her to bed, but she was so quiet, I just left her in her chair.

WITNESS. And then?

SELENA. I went to bed.

WITNESS. Did you sleep?

SELENA. *(Smiling.)* Oh, yes. Lord, yes. I slept, I can't remember sleeping like that. Straight through the morning. I don't even think I dreamed, that's how deep I was sleeping.

WITNESS. And when you woke up?

SELENA. I got dressed and I made us some coffee.

WITNESS. 'Us'?

SELENA. Yes. Me and Esther. I always brought her coffee first thing. She didn't ever drink much of it, but I think she liked the smell. She recognized the smell.

WITNESS. And you brought her her coffee?

SELENA. Yes. I did. And you know, as soon as I saw her, I knew. I knew she was passed on.

WITNESS. What did you do?

SELENA. I put my hand on her forehead. And I jumped. She was so frigid.

WITNESS. What were you expecting?

SELENA. Esther was always warmer than usual. But I could see she was gone. I cried so hard, my sides hurt me and I couldn't breathe.

WITNESS. You cried?

SELENA. Oh, for days. After all, she was my mother.

(Lights blaze white. The WITNESSES reset the stage. ESTHER is wheeled off. VIVIAN and her brother JOHN come down to the table. SELENA makes herself look pretty. They are all laughing. SELENA is effervescent, almost girlish in her behavior.)

JOHN. And the bartender looks at him and says, you know sometimes Superman, you have the worst sense of humor.

(They ALL laugh harder.)

VIVIAN. And so do you have the worst sense of I don't know if I can call it humor.

SELENA. It's a funny story.

JOHN. Thank you, ma'am.

VIVIAN. Oh, you will laugh at anything.

JOHN. My sister never appreciated my sense of the ridiculous.

SELENA. I could never tell a story. I used to try to remember them for my mother, so it would give me something to say to her—she had multiple strokes, she couldn't really talk—but I just didn't have the knack or the good memory or whatever it is that makes a good story good, I was forever hemming and hawing and never getting it right ...

VIVIAN. Well, listen to the girl talk!

SELENA. Oh, I'm sorry. Am I jabbermouthing?

JOHN. Nothing of the kind. You're just making conversation.

VIVIAN. Oh, is that what is it? Where I come from it's called flirtation.

SELENA. I'll clear the dishes.

VIVIAN. Oooh, I've embarrassed her.

JOHN. You could embarrass a pig in a mud hole.

VIVIAN. Oh, get on outside and have a cigarette. Give your lungs another breath of cancer.

(VIVIAN pushes JOHN downstage.)

JOHN. Alright. I'm going.

VIVIAN. If you keep your mouth shut, we might let you have some dessert. Selena made a pie for us.

SELENA. You don't have to eat it.

JOHN. Oh yes I do. And I will, too.

(JOHN goes. VIVIAN takes SELENA's hands.)

VIVIAN. Leave them. I'll get them.

SELENA. No.

VIVIAN. You know why I tease you like I do?

SELENA. No. Why?

VIVIAN. Because I love you like my own family. And when I see you so changed. So happy. It makes my heart want to wet its pants. Oh, honey, I think he likes you.

SELENA. Who?

VIVIAN. My brother. That's who. And don't tell me it wasn't some kind of divine providence that brought him back to this town at this moment.

SELENA. At *what* moment?

VIVIAN. It's never too late, you know. That's what they say and "they" generally know.

SELENA. *(Laughs.)* Vivian, you are ... Well, I don't know *what* you are, but as soon as I *do* know, I'm going to tell you. Believe me.

VIVIAN. Go on outside. I'll clear. Go on. Go on. At your age, you can't afford to waste another minute.

(VIVIAN hugs SELENA and pushes her toward JOHN. Then she clears the dishes and exits. SELENA takes a bottle of pills from her pocket. She swallows a few. She puts the bottle away. Then she takes the bottle out again and swallows a few more pills. Then she moves toward JOHN.)

JOHN. She's something, isn't she?

SELENA. Yes, she is.

JOHN. She'll say anything that comes into her head. Always been that way. From the time we were kids growing up.

SELENA. She has a good heart.

JOHN. And an evil mind.

SELENA. No harm done.

JOHN. Was it true?

SELENA. What? Was what true?

JOHN. What she said. Were you flirting with me?

SELENA. *(Laughs.)* Well, it runs in the family, I guess, saying what's on your mind.

JOHN. I guess it does. Except I usually have a purpose to what I say.

SELENA. Maybe it's just the full moon having an influence.

JOHN. Now that's not true.

SELENA. What isn't?

JOHN. That full moon nonsense.

SELENA. Why not?

JOHN. It's a fallacy. That's why not. One of those things people are always saying that just ain't so.

SELENA. How do *you* know it ain't so?

JOHN. Because they proved it.

SELENA. They proved the moon?

JOHN. No. They counted up all the accidents and the murders and the suicides and the numbers of people running to the emergency rooms in hospitals—and it turns out there ain't no difference between what happens on a day when there is a full moon and a day when there isn't.

SELENA. Maybe it ain't so. But it's still a notion. It's an idea. And it's a way of understanding things. Especially things you can't explain.

JOHN. But it's not true. You can't settle for what's not true. Same as people saying that no two snowflakes are alike. Or if you crack your knuckles you get arthritis. Because it's been proven that you *can* find two identical snowflakes and it can *not* be proven that cracking knuckles makes your bones sick.

SELENA. *(Enjoying this.)* Alright. Alright. I give up.

JOHN. So there.

SELENA. What else do they say that ain't so?

JOHN. Well, here's a good one. They say that a woman

reaches her sexual peak at around thirty years old—now don't be embarrassed.

SELENA. *(She is.)* I'm not.

JOHN. And they say a man reaches his peak much earlier. About eighteen years old.

SELENA. Well, how about that.

JOHN. Now do you know how they came to these conclusions?

SELENA. I can't imagine.

JOHN. I bet you can.

SELENA. *(Laughs.)* I can *not.*

JOHN. Well, I'll tell you.

SELENA. That's what I was afraid of.

JOHN. They took a survey.

SELENA. Oh, dear.

JOHN. They took a survey and they asked people how many orgasms they were having.

SELENA. Oh. I see.

JOHN. You know—one a day, two a day, four a week, once a month. Like that.

SELENA. I see. Yes. I do see.

JOHN. And based on these findings, they made their conclusions. In other words, men have more orgasms at the age of eighteen and women have the most number or orgasms at age thirty.

SELENA. Ah.

JOHN. But I ask you, what does that mean? And is that a sexual peak or an *orgasmic* peak? Because I happen to think there's a difference. You see?

SELENA. I wonder if Vivian needs any help?

JOHN. Because first of all, you can have an orgasm alone. Can't you? Now an eighteen year old boy, all alone in his room, pulling on his pud, you know, playing with himself eight, nine times a day is not my idea of a sexual giant.

SELENA. Please, Mr. Baines ...

JOHN. John.

SELENA. Please, John, you say you always have a purpose in what you say. What is your purpose in saying these things to me?

JOHN. That's a fair question. I guess I'm trying to impress you. Not only with my intelligence and my ability to converse in a charming manner. But also with my understanding of a few basic human principles. One of which is this: that no matter how old or young a person may be—and no matter what the surveys may say—a person still needs companionship and warmth and a person still needs love of every kind and a sexual peak may have more to do with how great that need is as much as it has to do with anything else.

(WITNESSES begin to sing. JOHN offers his hand. He and SELENA dance slowly.)

SELENA. *(As she dances.)* We saw each other for almost two months.

WITNESS. Every day?

SELENA. And just about every night, too. My need was very great.

WITNESS. This was a happy time?

SELENA. I think so. Yes. I was nervous still. I kept thinking, is this sinful, what I'm doing? Is this wrong? I was ashamed and at the same time, I was ... well, I don't know.

WITNESS. Were you still taking medication?

SELENA. Valium. Transzene. Nembutol. Phenobarbital. And, at that time, I think I started the Elavil. So my memory of all of it is a little ... well, unclear. But I think I can say it was a happy time.

JOHN. I retired once ... worst thing I could have done. Retire. Nearly killed me. Then I took this job caretaking over at the school. That made the difference. Not the job so much. But the kids. You see that? It was the kids. Not that I have anything to do with them, but just that they're there. My own daughter was long gone. Married. Being around those kids, I felt—well, I *didn't* feel so old and finished.

SELENA. I see what you mean.

JOHN. Like anything else. You give up on it, it gives up on you. If you *think* you're too old for something, then you *are*. Of course, you're young yet. But, still, it's a danger of the mind. So if I want to do something and I hear a voice saying, you can't do that, then, hell, I have to do it.

SELENA. I can see that, too.

JOHN. Well, then, what do you say?

SELENA. About what?

JOHN. Selena, I want to marry you.

(Lights change. Music stops abruptly. VIVIAN enters with a pile of magazines. JOHN exits. WITNESSES exit. SELENA joins VIVIAN at the table. As they flip through the magazines ...)

VIVIAN. I don't see why you can't wear white.

SELENA. I couldn't.

VIVIAN. Why not?

SELENA. It wouldn't be right.

VIVIAN. Oh, these things don't mean what they used to mean. Nobody's going to worry about whether or not you are some kind of virgin. If that's what you're thinking.

SELENA. No.

VIVIAN. I just think first time out of the gate, you should wear white. Now if this was the third or fourth time, then I think a girl is pushing the outside of the envelope.

SELENA. Maybe if it's just a dress. You know, not a full length gown.

VIVIAN. This is nice, look at this.

SELENA. Oh, can you see me in that?!

VIVIAN. Yes.

SELENA. Is that a hat?

VIVIAN. No. I think it's just hair.

SELENA. Does it hurt?

VIVIAN. Well, you know you don't have to take these pictures word for word. You just get an idea and then we can go into town and have something sort of similar sewn up.

SELENA. We don't have money for that.

VIVIAN. Oh, it don't cost nothing.

SELENA. Well, it'd have to be *less* than nothing before we could afford it.

VIVIAN. There's got to be *something* to make this day special. We ain't having a big reception. We ain't having a big ceremony.

SELENA. It'll just be special for what it is. That's all *(The magazine.)* Oh, look at these rooms. Honest to God, do people live like this?

VIVIAN. You're asking me?

SELENA. You think I could make the house look anything like this?

VIVIAN. No.

SELENA. *(Full of energy and hope.)* I'd like to pass through it with a big bucket of paint and white wash every ceiling, wall and floor and nook and cranny. I'd like to throw out every stick of furniture, every couch and cushion and all the dust that you can't beat out of them. And the smell and the damp and the useless sets of cracked dishes and the flatware that ain't got an ounce of silver left on them and the yellow linen. I'd like to throw it all out. And rip down the curtains and the wallpaper and the plaster. I'd like to make it all new and clean and fresh like fresh air. And bright. And full of light. *(And then she breaks down.)* Oh, Vivian. I can't do this. I can't do any of this ...

VIVIAN. Selena ...

SELENA. Look at me. What are we talking about?

VIVIAN. Honey, you're just a bundle of nerves. That's all. That's normal.

SELENA. Look at these pictures. Look at these houses. Look at these recipes, look at that table—that don't even look like food to me. You ever seen food laid out on a plate like that? You ever seen what *I* cook? Or worse, you ever tasted it?

VIVIAN. These are just dream pictures. Pictures for dreaming. Nobody lives like this really.

SELENA. He's going to be disappointed. He can't help but be.

VIVIAN. That ain't so.

SELENA. Oh, yes it is. I don't know what he sees in me. What is it? *What is it he's seeing when he looks at me*?!

VIVIAN. I can't answer that. But he's seen a good part of you already and he don't seem disappointed in that.

SELENA. (Shocked.) He told you that?

VIVIAN. What? That he ain't disappointed? Well, not in so many ...

SELENA. He told you that he and I ... that we ...

VIVIAN. That you been sleeping together? There's nothing wrong with that. You're grown up people.

SELENA. You have to excuse me, Vivian. I have to go out.

VIVIAN. Oh, me and my mouth ...

SELENA. I'll call you tomorrow.

VIVIAN. Will you just listen to me for half a ...

SELENA. I'll speak to you tomorrow.

(SELENA comes downstage. VIVIAN exits. A WITNESS stands in his place and plays a SECOND DRUGGIST. Both he and SELENA face front when they speak.)

DRUGGIST #2. These are pretty strong.

SELENA. They're for my mother. She doesn't take them regularly. She doesn't take them hardly at all. I just like to have them there for her. Just in case.

DRUGGIST #2. And you just had them refilled.

SELENA. I know, I don't know where the others got to. I suspect I must have put them away somewhere. I keep them in those little pill containers. It's just lucky I kept the empty bottle with the label on it.

(A third WITNESS plays another DRUGGIST.)

DRUGGIST #3. Well this should keep you a while, Miss Goodall.

SELENA. Baines. Mrs. Baines. Would you put Mrs. Baines on the label.

DRUGGIST #3. Is that you?

SELENA. Yes. I'm about to be married.

DRUGGIST #3. I see.

SELENA. Almost any day now.

DRUGGIST #3. Oh. Well, congratulations.

SELENA. Well, thank you. It was a surprise to me, too.

(They laugh. Another WITNESS stands and plays another DRUGGIST.)

DRUGGIST #4. Is this you? Are you Mrs. John Baines?

SELENA. No. That's the woman I work for.

DRUGGIST #4. Well, I don't recall filling this for her.

SELENA. Maybe I misunderstood which drugstore she meant. She's in such terrible pain ...

DRUGGIST #4. I understand.

SELENA. ... sometimes she confuses things.

(Another WITNESS stands.)

DRUGGIST #5. I see.

SELENA. And she spilled the entire bottle into the sink. And I just had the prescription refilled.

DRUGGIST #5. Yes. I can see that. But all the same ...

SELENA. (Babbling.) And I ran all the way back to the other drugstore. But they close early on Monday night. So I didn't know what to do. I need to get these tonight—you don't know what it's like getting her through the night without her medication. She suffers so much. And to watch her suffer and be helpless is another kind of torture altogether.

DRUGGIST #4. Yes.

DRUGGIST #5. Yes.

DRUGGIST #3. I see.

DRUGGIST #2. Yes.

SELENA. So finally I looked in the yellow pages and that's how I found you even though it meant coming clear across town, I just had to hope and pray that you would be able to help me ...

DRUGGIST #5. Yes. Alright. Alright.

DRUGGIST #4. I guess it's alright.

DRUGGIST #3. I can do this for you.

SELENA. Thank you.

DRUGGIST #2. There you are. All set.

SELENA. Oh, thank you.

DRUGGIST #4. Goodnight.

SELENA. Goodnight.

DRUGGIST #3. Good day.

SELENA. Good-bye.

DRUGGIST #5. Good-bye now.

SELENA. Good-bye.

DRUGGIST #2. Good-bye.

(Lights change. WITNESSES all sit. SELENA walks unsteadily to the television and turns it on. She is completely stoned— dry mouth, heavy eyes, precarious balance.)

SELENA. Thank you. I do appreciate ... I do ... for your help and ... for helping ... me to be ... *(She listens to the T.V.)* Have mercy on me. Oh, God. Have mercy on me ...

WITNESSES. *(Hard, loud and fast.)* Have mercy upon me, Oh, God, according to your loving kindness ...

SELENA. In your kindness ...

WITNESSES. Pray with us, sinners.

SELENA. Pray with me ...

WITNESSES. According to the multitudes of your tender mercies ...

SELENA. ... your tender mercy.

WITNESSES. Blot out my transgressions.

SELENA. Wash me from my iniquity and cleanse me from my sin. I know these words.

WITNESSES. ... for I acknowledge my transgressions and my sin is always before me.

SELENA. *(Simultaneous.)* And my sin is always before me.

WITNESSES. Behold I was brought forth in iniquity and in sin my mother conceived me.

SELENA. *(Growing angry.)* I know the words but they are not easy. I know that you desire the truth in the most inward parts of me. But it is not easy. And in the hidden part, you will make me to know wisdom. But the hidden part is hidden and I cannot see it. And there are parts I do see but you make me ashamed. And I cannot rejoice in who I am. I cannot sing my life. I cannot dance free of that unholy pain or shake it out of me. *(She spits out the words, pulling some of her clothing off.)* 'Purge me and I shall be clean; wash me and I shall be whiter than snow.' I know the words, but I can't hear them. I know you are here. But I cannot see you. I wait for you to come, but you never do. Please, help me. *(She sings.)* Please help me, I'm falling.

(She laughs and falls to the floor.)

WITNESSES. Deliver me from the guilt of bloodshed, Oh, God, the God of my salvation, and my tongue shall sing aloud of your righteousness.

SELENA. Oh, Lord, open my lips. Open my mouth. Come inside. Come inside me. Make me good.

(Blackout. When the lights come up, JOHN is alone on stage. SELENA enters. She is very groggy. It's an effort to stand up. She moves toward JOHN.)

JOHN. Well, there you are.

SELENA. Oh, my.

JOHN. How are you feeling?

SELENA. I don't know. I feel a little bit like I been run over by a truck on a four lane highway.

JOHN. You been sleeping ...

SELENA. Yes. I slept a long time, didn't I?

JOHN. You been asleep a long time.

SELENA. My head is all fuzzy.

JOHN. Yes.

SELENA. I don't know what happened to me.

JOHN. You were on the floor.

SELENA. I was?

JOHN. You were unconscious on the floor.

SELENA. I don't know ...

JOHN. Then you were saying things.

SELENA. It's so peculiar.

JOHN. I couldn't understand most of it.

SELENA. What could I be saying?

JOHN. Prayer things. Things from the bible.

SELENA. What happened to my arm?

JOHN. You had your sewing needles. You were ripping at hour arm with them, making crosses with your blood ...

SELENA. Oh, John ...

JOHN. I never seen anything like that ...

SELENA. I was alright this morning ...

JOHN. ... spitting words like that.

SELENA. Then all of a sudden ...

JOHN. ... and pushing me away ...

SELENA. ... this fever come over me ...

JOHN. ... slapping at me with your fist ...

SELENA. It was a fever.

JOHN. I had blood everywhere.

SELENA. It made me so sick. I don't remember ever feeling that sick before. Like one of those twenty-four hour viruses—only double. And so fast. One minute I was up, the next minute, well, I don't know ... *(Pause.)* I put some water on. I thought I'd make us some coffee.

JOHN. Have I failed you, Selena?

SELENA. What? What do you mean? How do you mean?

JOHN. Have I disappointed you in some way?

SELENA. No.

JOHN. It's a long way to go to love somebody. I don't know that I have the time left—or even the inclination—to go that long a way again. But I do respect you. And I would like us to be friends as long as we were together.

SELENA. I would like that, too.

JOHN. And even if we didn't get married ... Well.

SELENA. Even if ... ?!

JOHN. Even if ... No matter. I would hope that we would still be friends.

SELENA. Well, yes, but ... Yes, we would.

JOHN. Good. Then, can you tell a friend—what are these?

(JOHN takes several handfuls of prescription pill bottles from his pocket and puts them on the table.)

SELENA. Those are pills. Those are medicine.

JOHN. Are you ill, Selena?

SELENA. No. Those were Esther's. Those were for my mother. You know, after she passed on, I just never got around to throwing them away. Where did you find them?

JOHN. Some of these have your own name on them.

SELENA. Yes, well I used to do that ...

JOHN. And some of them use my name as if you were my wife.

SELENA. Yes ...

JOHN. And more than half of them were prescribed in the past six months, after your mother died. I need to have some kind of explanation here. Or else I will begin to imagine things that are far worse than the truth.

SELENA. Yes.

JOHN. I don't need that explanation now. But in your own time. Meanwhile, I have taken all pill bottles in the house and I have emptied the contents into the toilet.

(Pause.)

SELENA. I'll get the coffee.

(SELENA pours two cups of coffee. Then she reaches into her panties and pulls out a bottle of pills. She takes several pills. The WITNESSES enter and take their places.
A telephone rings. SELENA speaks as if on the phone. A WIT-NESS brings her a cup of coffee. Another WITNESS brings her the box of arsenic. As she speaks, she puts the poison into the coffee and gives it to JOHN. He drinks it.)

SELENA. (Cont.) Hello? Oh, Vivian. Hello. Uh-huh. Well, I'm fine. How are you? I haven't seen you in I don't know how long. Oh, yes? Yes. Well, it's been raining over here, too. Yes. Well, no. Not today. It ain't raining today. But yesterday, I think. Didn't it rain yesterday? Or was that the day before? I'm so busy with the wedding plans. *(Phone rings again.)* Oh, hi Viv. Oh yes. Yes, he is. But he's lying down. No, he's not going to work anymore. *(Near tears.)* Fever, now. Terrible fever and such pain. It just gets worse and worse. I'm so worried, Viv. I'm sick myself for worrying and I don't know, really. I don't know what to do ... *(A WITNESS wheels in a cot. JOHN is in pain. He gets onto the cot.)* He won't have a doctor. I said the same thing, but he won't have one. He won't have anything to do with a doctor. You know what he's like. Yes ... Yes ...

(WITNESSES sing a wedding song and recite the wedding ceremony.)

WITNESS. Dearly beloved, we are gathered together ...

(VIVIAN enters wearing a hat and carrying a veil and a corsage for SELENA.)

VIVIAN. I brought these. I didn't know if it was a good idea.

SELENA. They're so pretty. Do you think I should?

VIVIAN. I honestly don't know.

SELENA. This is certainly not the wedding we were dreaming about.

VIVIAN. No. Not at all. But in this life, you grabs what you can get.

SELENA. Yes. That's right. Isn't it? We just reach for heaven and just hope that heaven will lend a hand.

WITNESS. ... in the name of our Lord, Jesus Christ, to join in holy matrimony ...

(SELENA goes to JOHN, takes his hand.)

VIVIAN. It was a beautiful ceremony. In its own way, of course. You could still smell the sick room—the ammonia and the disinfectant. And that terrible feeling of hope that you get at a wedding—well, the whole idea of a future was just not present. But in the center of all that—somewhere apart from all the heavy gloom of it—somewhere in their own time and in their own way, there was John and Selena holding on to each other's hand. It was like a beautiful white thing, a beautiful white bird had landed in hell somehow and spread its wings and made hell holy for just a minute.

And I thought to myself, well, the world is never what you expect. And expecting it to be anything at all is probably the biggest mistake a person can make. I love Selena with my whole heart. And I think sometimes I wanted her to be happy even more than I wanted myself to be happy. I wanted her to open up to the joy of living, to let go of her fear and feel the love that God allows even his most crippled creation. Which I guess is what she was. And how I didn't know is a great part of the mystery. *(WITNESSES come down to JOHN. They change cot to hospital gurney. They wheel JOHN off stage. SELENA goes with him.)* The pain got worse and worse. By the time John consented finally to let us take him to the hospital, they had to strap him to the bed. The pain was that bad. He was twisting and pulling and ripping at his insides, biting on his own tongue so his mouth was always bleeding, smacking his head on the headboard so he would lose consciousness and not feel the pain. I prayed for him to die. There wasn't a doctor there who had any idea in hell what was wrong with him. There wasn't any kind of hope. So I prayed for it.

(SELENA comes down to VIVIAN and takes her hands.)

SELENA. He's gone, Viv.
VIVIAN. Oh, Jesus, forgive me.
SELENA. He's just gone.
VIVIAN. *(Comforting SELENA.)* Honey, I'm sorry.
SELENA. Let's sing, Viv. Sing that hymn with me. I feel so lonely and lost. I think my heart is just sinking down to die.

(VIVIAN starts to sing a hymn. SELENA sings with her. Lights blaze white. The singing stops. The stage is reset. The WIT-NESSES sit in the chairs. One WITNESS comes down to play MRS. FENNEL. She brings a baby carriage with her. As she looks through letters of recommendation ...)

MRS. FENNEL. Well, these are impressive.
SELENA. Thank you.
MRS. FENNEL. *Very* impressive.
SELENA. I'm a good worker.
MRS. FENNEL. I guess so.
SELENA. I've taken care of people all my life. And now I do it professionally.
MRS. FENNEL. Mostly older people.
SELENA. That's true. Since my husband passed away ...

MRS. FENNEL. When was that?

SELENA. Oh, four—five years now. Since then, it's what I've been doing. It chases away the loneliness.

MRS. FENNEL. Yes. I guess so.

SELENA. You make your own kind of family. And I was living in with most of them. Most of them, as they got on, were too sick to take care of themselves. So then I would move into their homes and take care of them until they passed on or didn't need me anymore—whatever.

MRS. FENNEL. It's hard with old people.

SELENA. Yes. More often than not, just when you start getting close, just when you really get to know each other, well ...

MRS. FENNEL. Gone. I know.

SELENA. Yes. That's why I was interested in this position. Not just because it's such a fine home. And such a good salary.

MRS. FENNEL. A baby is a very different situation.

SELENA. *(Laughs.)* Well, I should hope so.

MRS. FENNEL. I mean, if you haven't had any experience ...

SELENA. Oh. I see what you mean. But ... well, I have. I have had experience.

MRS. FENNEL. *(Looking at letters.)* I don't see anything...

SELENA. No, I mean my *own* children. I've had the experience of my own children.

MRS. FENNEL. Oh, I didn't realize ...

SELENA. Yes. Didn't I say that? Didn't I say that I had children of my own?

MRS. FENNEL. No.

SELENA. Oh. Well, three. Yes. Two girls and a boy. They're all grown up now. But I raised them all by myself.

MRS. FENNEL. How do you mean?

SELENA. Being a single mother ...

MRS. FENNEL. But I thought your husband only died a few years ago.

SELENA. *(A beat.)* My second husband. That was my second husband. My first died right after the children were born.

MRS. FENNEL. Good timing.

SELENA. What?

MRS. FENNEL. I'm sorry. But they do always seem to go at the worst time.

SELENA. Did *your* husband pass away?

MRS. FENNEL. No. He didn't die. No. *(She laughs.)* He's just gone.

SELENA. Oh. I'm sorry.

MRS. FENNEL. Nothing to be sorry about. Believe me. Well. Selena. Let's give it a try. It may only be a few months. I'm trying to get back to work. I just need some help until I can establish a routine ...

SELENA. *(Smiles.)* Oh. I don't know. Once you see how useful I can be—I mean, once I start, people generally have a hard time getting rid of me.

(WITNESSES enter and watch SELENA. MRS. FENNEL exits. SELENA takes charge of the baby carriage. She sings a nursery rhyme to the baby—like a lullaby.)

SELENA. 'Twinkle, twinkle, little star
How I wonder what you are'

END OF ACT I

ACT II

(As before, SELENA is with the baby carriage. VIVIAN is with her.)

VIVIAN. Is she asleep?

SELENA. I think so.

VIVIAN. Thank God.

SELENA. I know.

VIVIAN. She still feeling poorly?

SELENA. Yeah. At first they thought it was the colic. But now they just don't know.

VIVIAN. Let me see her.

SELENA. She looks so peaceful. You know sometimes I sit, watching her, and I cannot take my eyes away. I see her breathe and I imagine the smallness of her lungs taking in the little bites of air—every part of her so small ...

VIVIAN. It's funny that both of us never had children. Isn't it?

SELENA. Well, speak for yourself.

VIVIAN. Well, I do, generally. Maybe you never wanted any and I always said I didn't want any—but I did.

SELENA. It's a big commitment, but you just do it. And if you had honest to god wanted them them you would have had them.

VIVIAN. Well, listen to you. The mother of us all. It wasn't that long ago I used to think you never ever *looked* below your waist. I used to see you taking showers with your slip on—like Catholic nuns.

SELENA. Now don't start on the nuns.

VIVIAN. Well, it's true.

SELENA. God will punish you.

VIVIAN. Punish me for what? I ain't done anything my whole life.

SELENA. Punish you for every third word that comes out of your mouth.

VIVIAN. Words is words. Most of them don't even have a thought behind them. I'm talking about what I *done*. What deeds have I done?

SELENA. I don't know *what* you're saying now.

VIVIAN. Oh, we *are* like a couple of nuns. Worse, even. Withering away. I would be ashamed to face God and say this is what I have to show for my life. For all the life that you gave me. For all the life that I used up—this is what I have to show. See me standing there in a house dress with my empty hands stretched out ...

SELENA. Why are you saying this? Stop now.

VIVIAN. And the only people I ever loved were my brother who died anyway and that silly old maid who married him ...

SELENA. Oh, Vivian.

VIVIAN. And did anyone ever love me? Was anyone ever there to open their arms to me, anyone who could see the hurt and the terrible being long so long, just open their arms and wrap me up in a little comfort. "—a little comfort at the cold end of the day." I don't think so. I don't think there was ever anybody who did that for me—or I think I would have remembered. I'm *sure* I would have remembered.

(SELENA wants to open her arms and comfort VIVIAN—but she can't.)

VIVIAN. Well ...

SELENA. Yes.

VIVIAN. I don't know what that was all about.

SELENA. It's the presence of children. Or the absence.

VIVIAN. I suppose. Yes.

SELENA. It pulls at the heart.

VIVIAN. Well, too late now.

SELENA. 'Higher than a house, higher than a tree. Oh, whatever can that be?'

VIVIAN. What?

SELENA. Guess. Guess. It's a riddle. You have to guess.

VIVIAN. Oh, for God's sake.

SELENA. Higher than a house, higher than a tree. Oh, whatever can that be?

VIVIAN. I don't get it.

SELENA. A star. It's a star.

VIVIAN. *What's* a star?

SELENA. The answer. The answer to the riddle. I know a hundred of them. I do them every morning with the baby. She don't know at all what I'm saying—but she smiles and makes sounds like she's trying to speak. And I think of Esther. I think how much getting old is just like turning into a baby because that's all Esther was at the end..

VIVIAN. Honey, don't dwell on the past.

SELENA. I'm not at all. My sights are glued to the future. And so should yours.

VIVIAN. What future?

SELENA. Oh, I don't mean twenty years from now. I mean next week. Tomorrow. This afternoon. You don't know what the next five minutes have in store.

VIVIAN. I can pretty much guess.

SELENA. Don't be that way.

VIVIAN. Alright. Alright.

SELENA. Life is precious. Every life. Every minute of every life. Every dark and terrible part of every dark and terrible life. God must be such a fool.

VIVIAN. Selena, what are you talking about?

SELENA. Not to know in all his wisdom how hard a life can be ...

VIVIAN. Now you're agreeing with me.

SELENA. ... how dark the darkness can get. When my first husband died and left me with those poor children—it was all I could do to keep my head above water. But the human spirit is resilient—despite everything. And we survived ...

VIVIAN. I lost the thread here ...

SELENA. Alright, we never lived like kings. But I provided for them. They never knew from want of anything essential and they grew into the finest, most beautiful young people—course, I'm prejudiced, because they're my own. But if you could see them ...

VIVIAN. If I could see who? Is this another riddle?

(VIVIAN is confounded. As SELENA speaks she takes out a baby's milk bottle, takes the top off, takes a small jar of white powder from the carriage, opens it, sprinkles some white powder into the milk.)

SELENA. Oh, Vivian, don't make me sad. I can't be sad. I wake up every day knowing that this child is waiting for me, needing me to take care of her—and my heart jumps up like a cherry bomb and explodes with happiness. *(She laughs.)* That's a funny way to put it, isn't it?

VIVIAN. Selena, what children are you talking about?

SELENA. *(Playful.)*
'Poor little children
Whose names I don't know
Were stolen away
On a fine summer's day'

VIVIAN. Selena, come on now, stop this and answer me.

SELENA.
'And left in a wood
As I've heard people say ...

And when it was night
So sad was their plight'
VIVIAN. Selena, stop it. Please just talk to me a minute.
SELENA.
'The sun it went down
And the moon gave no light
They sobbed and they sighed
And they lay down and died ...'

(VIVIAN grabs her and tries to shake her.)

VIVIAN. Selena, what's this?

(VIVIAN picks up the jar of white powder.)

SELENA. Oh, just a little something.
VIVIAN. A little something for what?
SELENA.
'And when they were dead
The robins so red
Mournfully whistled
All the day long
And this was their song ...'
VIVIAN. Did you put this in her milk? What are you putting in her milk?
SELENA. 'Poor babes in the wood! Poor babes in the wood...'
VIVIAN. Selena ...
SELENA. 'Oh, don't you remember ...'
VIVIAN. *(Taking the bottle from the baby.)* Selena—what is this?! *What is in this milk*?!

(Slowly, SELENA looks at the jar of poison. Then the milk bottle. She starts to shake.
Lights Change. Flash bulbs explode. Two WITNESSES enter as NEWSCASTERS. ESTHER's voice is recorded. SELENA

is strapped onto a gurney.)

NEWSCASTER #1. Robeson County was shocked today by the arrest of Selena Goodall Baines for the attempted murder of a 10-month-old child who was in her care ...

SELENA/ESTHER. *(Very unsteady.)* "Oh, lord, rebuke me not in thy wrath; neither chasten me in thy hot displeasure. For thine arrows stick fast in me, and thy hand presseth me sore ..."

NEWSCASTER #1. The suspect was moved from the county jail to the State Hospital for observation ...

SELENA. Do you have any aspirin? Could I have an aspirin?

NEWSCASTER #1. ... And for tests in relation to a charge of possible illegal procurement of prescription drugs.

SELENA. I need to have something ... I don't feel right.

NEWSCASTER #2. Police have been unable to ascertain any motive for the crime. Although the horrifying act would seem to be drug related.

SELENA/ESTHER. ' ... for my iniquities are gone over my head; as a heavy burden, they are too heavy for me ...'

SELENA. I cannot bear it. Don't leave me here like this.

NEWSCASTER #2. Selena Goodall is currently at State Hospital in Raleigh, North Carolina, undergoing a detoxification program ...

SELENA. ... My loins are filled with a loathsome disease and there is no soundness in my flesh ...

NEWSCASTER #2. Authorities have been unable to question the suspect who remains in a confused and delirious state...

SELENA. *(Losing all control.)* I am feeble and sore broken; I need to have something. You need to give me something.

Lord, lord, lord, all my desire is before thee. Listen to me. Please. I can't breathe. I can't. My mouth hurts. My heart panteth, my strength fails me; as for the light of my eyes, it is also gone from me. I can't see. I can't see.

Please! Please! Give me something—*please*! My eyes! I

can't see. *(A WITNESS enters and gives her and injection. She grows quieter. ESTHER walks down to SELENA. This is a dream.)* Hear me, Oh Lord. I am ready to stop now ...

ESTHER. *(Wipes SELENA's brow.)* Shhh ... Sleep now. You're asleep.

SELENA. ... my sorrow is always before me ...

ESTHER. Shhh ... You don't need to pray now. You don't need to pray now or ever again.

SELENA. ... my enemies are strong ...

ESTHER. You have no enemies. Not anymore.

SELENA. I cannot fight them, Esther. I can't ...

ESTHER. You don't need to fight. Not now. Sleep.

SELENA. ... they multiply.

ESTHER. They disappear. They are all gone now, those enemies. Let them go.

(JOHN walks down to SELENA. During the following, he un- straps her.)

SELENA. Oh, John. I am so tired

JOHN. Then *be* tired. That's alright.

SELENA. I am too tired to fight.

JOHN. The fight is over now.

SELENA. Over?

JOHN. Oh, yes.

SELENA. Have I lost then? Esther! Have I lost?

ESTHER. Lost? I don't know. But you are tired and the battle is over.

SELENA. I will declare mine iniquity; I will be sorry for my sin ...

JOHN. *(With good humor.)* Oh, listen to you—always so damned important, every little thing you say, do or even think about in passing, blown up out of all proportion. Nobody cares about your sin. You tell me what sin is—or show it to me—or even just show me the *consequences* of sin—then I'll believe there is such a thing ...

SELENA. Oh, you're just saying this, trying to make me feel better.

JOHN. Why would I want to make you feel better? You took my life ...

SELENA. Oh, John ...

JOHN. You took it slowly and painfully.

SELENA. Did I do that?

JOHN. Oh, yes. And your mother's life, too.

ESTHER. Don't you listen to him, Selena. You're a good girl.

SELENA. I'm a good girl.

JOHN. Well, I never said you weren't. But all the same ...

ESTHER. You're a good, good girl.

SELENA. But I must have done something to have them treat me so bad ...

JOHN. The truth is—nobody's perfect.

SELENA. I'm a good girl.

ESTHER. That's right—no matter how far they drag you down into the muck and the mire, no matter how soiled you may become.

SELENA. I'm a good girl, John.

JOHN. Go on. Just go on. You'll be alright now.

ESTHER. Go on. Good-bye.

JOHN. Good-bye now.

SELENA. No. Don't go ...

ESTHER. Go on. I'll say good-bye now.

SELENA. Don't say good-bye ...

(One WITNESS enters to play the LAWYER.)

LAWYER. Mrs. Baines?

SELENA. Hello?

LAWYER. Would you like to sit down?

SELENA Would I ...

JOHN. Don't you fight them any more, Selena. You give in now. Give into the truth.

(SELENA walks down to the lawyer. She is very weak and confused. JOHN and ESTHER exit.)

LAWYER. Do you want to sit down?

SELENA. Oh. I don't think so.

LAWYER. Okay. Can I get you anything?

SELENA. *(Suspicious.)* I don't know. What is it that I need?

LAWYER. Well, a glass of water. Cup of coffee.

SELENA. *(Relieved.)* Oh. I see.

LAWYER. Whatever.

SELENA. Oh, no. No. That's alright. Thank you.

LAWYER. Okay. So.

SELENA. So?

LAWYER. Do you want to tell me what happened?

SELENA. What happened?

LAWYER. Yes.

SELENA. No. I mean, what *did* happen? Do *you* know? Are you here to tell me?

LAWYER. Well, I have the police report. But I'd prefer hearing this from you. Personally. That's why I'm here on a glorious Saturday morning with my pen in hand and my paper waiting.

SELENA. You're from the police.

LAWYER. Jesus. No. No, Mrs. Baines, I'm ...

SELENA. Excuse me. Please. I'm sorry, but would you not call me that? Would you not call me Mrs. Baines?

LAWYER. Alright, sure. But ... you are Mrs. Baines, aren't you? I'm not in the wrong cell, am I?

SELENA. No. But I wish you would call me Selena Goodall. I was never really Mrs. Baines. Never really.

LAWYER. Whatever. Just so I got the right person.

SELENA. Yes. You have the right person.

LAWYER. Good.

SELENA. If you're not from the police—who are you?

LAWYER. I'm your attorney, honey. Appointed by the court. I'm here to represent you in the case of the State of North Carolina versus Selena Goodall Baines.

SELENA. Oh.

LAWYER. Do you follow that?

SELENA. I think I'd like to sit down now. Is that alright?

LAWYER. Alright. Just take it easy. Jesus Christ almighty.

SELENA. Don't.

LAWYER. Don't what?

SELENA. Don't take the name of the Lord in vain. Please.

LAWYER. Well, fuck me.

SELENA. Or use profanity.

LAWYER. If that ain't the pot calling the kettle every name in the book ...

SELENA. Please.

LAWYER. Alright. Alright. I'm sorry. I know you're going through a lot here and I don't want to sound like a Pollyanna, but I don't really think you have too much to worry about. I don't think we'll ever go to trial on this one. You're a nice lady. Everybody says that. Even Mrs. Fennel, and she's the kid's mother. What everyone thinks is that you were under some stress and that, coupled with the prescription drugs— and that kind of addiction can happen to anybody—this is what we call temporary insanity which just means that you were not in control of your actions and therefore not responsible.

SELENA. I never meant to hurt anyone.

LAWYER. Of course not.

SELENA. I never felt anything but love for everyone.

LAWYER. Of course you did. And that baby is fine now. I don't think they even wanted to press charges except they all figured—they knew you needed to get help so nothing like this would happen again. That's all.

SELENA. Are you here to help me?

LAWYER. Well—yes. I guess you could say that.

SELENA. *(Taking his hand.)* Because I do *need* help now. And I thank you for it.

LAWYER. Uh ... you're welcome.

("WITNESSES take their places as "the court.")

PROSECUTOR. Mrs. Baines, could you explain to the court why you had this jar of rat poison in your possession.

(SELENA is still weak and very shaky. But she is also calm, courteous—even charming. She speaks to the lawyer at first. As the 'trial' emerges, she begins to address the 'court'— as do the other witnesses.)

SELENA. Oh, we had rats in the basement. It was so embarrassing. Esther was so humiliated.

PROSECUTOR. Esther?

SELENA. My mother. She said they were the eighth plague of Egypt sent to punish us.

PROSECUTOR. For what?

SELENA. For our wickedness. *(She laughs.)* That's what Esther believed. The eighth plague loose in the cellar multiplying in the darkness, gathering strength like an army, waiting to attack and vanquish us sinners who lived over their heads in pride. Glory, glory.

PROSECUTOR. Do you still live in your mother's house?

SELENA. Oh, no. Not for years and years.

PROSECUTOR. Then why did you still have this poison in your possession?

SELENA. They follow you. It don't matter where you live—how far you go to escape—this is what Esther believed— Your sins will find you. They will follow you and find you. That's what Esther believed.

PROSECUTOR. And do you believe that to be true?

SELENA. Well, I always did carry that poison with me— so I guess I didn't disbelieve it.

LAWYER. Selena, did you purchase that poison for the express purpose of feeding it to the Fennel baby?

SELENA. Oh, no. I loved that child. I would never do anything to hurt that child.

LAWYER. But you did hurt her.

SELENA. Yes. I did. But you see, Mrs. Fennel ...

MRS. FENNEL. I was going to let her go.

SELENA. ... she was going to let me go.

MRS. FENNEL. I was going to be working out of my home—I had everything pretty much under control by then ...

SELENA. I was there only six months.

MRS. FENNEL. And that's when the baby started getting sick ...

SELENA. I didn't give her hardly anything at all ...

MRS. FENNEL. So naturally I asked her to stay on.

SELENA. Just enough to ... well ...

LAWYER. Just enough to what?

SELENA. I wanted them to need me. So they wouldn't let me go. I was just learning to love them—I couldn't give them up so fast. So I only gave the baby just enough to make her a little sick ...

PROSECUTOR. But suppose you gave her too much? Let's forget for the moment that you put this child in pain and discomfort—suppose you had miscalculated and given her too much.

SELENA. I wouldn't have done that.

PROSECUTOR. How do you know that? How can you be sure?

SELENA. Because I knew. I knew the amount needed in proportion to the weight of the ... person.

PROSECUTOR. And how did you come by this kind of information?

SELENA. Well, I read it in books—there are medical books that have that kind of information in them.

PROSECUTOR. Books do not make a person an expert—not in *any* field of endeavor.

LAWYER. That's a statement—not a question.

PROSECUTOR. I'll rephrase, your honor—Did these medical books give you enough information on the subject of arsenic poisoning to make you an expert in the field of attempted murder and torture?

LAWYER. Your honor, please!

SELENA. It wasn't just the books ...

LAWYER. This behavior on the part of the prosecution ...

SELENA. I did have some experience.

PROSECUTOR. Experience at what?

LAWYER. Selena, you do not have to answer that question.

PROSECUTOR. Experience at what?

SELENA. I did know what I was doing. It was not haphazard.

PROSECUTOR. Because you had 'experience?'

SELENA. Yes. I knew how to take care of all my children.

PROSECUTOR. There were other children in your care?

SELENA. I called them children. I thought of them as children.

PROSECUTOR. So when you say 'children' you mean other patients or people who were in your care.

SELENA. Yes. That's right. There was Ruth Ann Fowler. Mary Margaret Stout. Peter John Newman. William Peterson...

PROSECUTOR. Yes. I see.

SELENA. Many more. And also including my mother, Esther Goodall, and my husband John Baines.

PROSECUTOR. Yes. You've had a great deal of experience taking care of the sick and the aged. But that is beside the point because unlike the child in question here, these people were not suffering from arsenic poisoning which you yourself inflicted.

SELENA. Oh, yes they were.

PROSECUTOR. I beg your pardon?

SELENA. Yes. I had given some to all of them. So you see, I did have experience. And I did know what I was doing.

(A commotion in the court. Everything overlaps here.)

LAWYER. Objection ...

PROSECUTOR. If the court please ...

NEWSCASTER. A shocking revelation in the trial of Selena Goodall Baines today ...

LAWYER. Your honor, this is new information ... I demand a recess ...

PROSECUTOR. Let the witness continue ...

NEWSCASTER. Selena say, there were others.

LAWYER. Under no circumstances ...

PROSECUTOR. Let her say what she has to say ...

NEWSCASTER. According to the accused herself, eight people died at her hands ...

LAWYER. Can we allow this testimony ...

PROSECUTOR. The issue here ...

LAWYER. Mrs. Baines is not on trial for ...

NEWSCASTER. Mrs. Baines admitted today to the killing of eight people including her husband and her mother.

PROSECUTOR. The issue here is whether or not the accused ...

LAWYER. She is not on trial for any other crimes except the attempted murder ...

PROSECUTOR. ... was temporarily insane.

LAWYER. ... of the Fennel child.

PROSECUTOR. If she knew what she was doing.

LAWYER. She did *not* know what she was doing ...

PROSECUTOR. In the interest of justice ...

LAWYER. In the interest of justice ...

WITNESSES. In the interest of justice ...

JUDGE. Order, please. Order. *(All the WITNESSES, including the LAWYER and PROSECUTOR, return to their places. Only the 'JUDGE' remains standing.)* Mrs. Baines. Let me understand. Are you telling the court that you administered poison to all the people who were in your care, who have been in your care for the past—how many years?

SELENA. Eleven years. But I never meant them any harm.

JUDGE. But you did administer poison.

SELENA. Yes.

JUDGE. And they did die.

SELENA. I'm sorry?

JUDGE. I say these people, these patients who were in your care—they did die.

SELENA. They did die. Yes ...

JUDGE. After you gave them this poison.
SELENA. Well ... yes, it was after ...
JUDGE. You gave them poison and they died.

(Long pause. Finally, it hits her.)

SELENA. Oh.

(SELENA is in shock. The fact of what she has done is finally clear to her.)

FOREMAN. On the charge of attempted murder of the child Lucinda Fennel, guilty. On the charge of murder in the first degree of William Peterson, guilty. For the murder of Anne Beuller, guilty.
SELENA. The first year was the hardest.
FOREMAN. For the murder of James Evert Anderson, guilty
SELENA. There was so little room.
FOREMAN. For the murder of Ruth Ann Fowler ...
SELENA. And air and light. I couldn't breathe.
FOREMAN. For the murder of Peter John Newman ... For the murder of Mary Margaret Stout ...
SELENA. Well, I could, but you know that terrible feeling of panic, like a cushion over your mouth, stopping the air? That used to come over me—oh, I don't know, two, three times a day.
FOREMAN. For the murder of her husband, John Baines, guilty.
SELENA. All the same, I felt safe in the prison. And protected. And for the first time in a long time, I was not looking after anyone. It was the other way around. And I did become accustomed to it all.
FOREMAN. For the murder of her mother, Esther Louise Goodall, guilty.
SELENA. But the worst of that time was not being able to

hide from myself and what I had done ...

(LAWYER comes down to SELENA.)

LAWYER. These things take time.
SELENA. I know that.
LAWYER. And you have to be patient, that's all. There are issues of addiction, molestation, depression that we have barely exploited ...
SELENA. But I don't want to have any more appeals made in my name. Can't I say that?
LAWYER. No.
SELENA. But it's what I want.
LAWYER. You can't say that.
SELENA. I want you to stop.
LAWYER. No. I can't do that. I can't.

(LAWYER goes.)

SELENA. The truth was ... there were eight living breathing human people—and they are gone now. Because of me. I had to live with that. And I didn't know how.

(The PREACHER enters.)

ˈPREACHER. Oh, children, are you in despair? Are you looking at the black hole of deep dark depression? Tipping over the edge, falling down into that blackness? Into the blackness of sin. Help me, help me, I'm falling.
SELENA. *(Absent minded.)* '... please help me, I'm falling...'
PREACHER. I'm falling. I'm falling—head over heels, ass over teakettle into the darkness. Yes! The light is disappearing. I cannot see my hand in front of my face. I cannot breathe without sucking the darkness into my nose, the mud of my disgrace in my mouth. I am choking on my own sins. I am lost in the dark. And I am ashamed.

SELENA. And then one morning on the radio ...

PREACHER. Now you listen to me, children. You put your ear close to the box and you listen to what I tell you. God sees you. You hear me? Say amen if you hear me. Amen, children. God sees you in the darkness. God sees you *through* the darkness. And he don't need no infra-red eye glasses neither. He sees you with his own eyes. God is looking at you *right now.* *Right now* he is looking into your unholy face. *Right now* he is looking deep into your soul. *Right now* looking into your shame. *Right now* he sees your sins. All of you. And he knows you. He knows you for the truth of what you are. And listen to this now, listen to what I'm telling you—he still loves you! *He loves you!* Loves you, loves you, looooooves you! And his only begotten son, Jesus Christ, he loves you too. Jesus loves you.

SELENA. Jesus loves you ...

PREACHER. Loves you—no matter what you do. All of you. All of you out there within the sound of my voice. In the fields and the factories, in the towering, tall buildings you have built to honor your own shame, in your rich houses, in your gutters, in your prisons.

Yes. Even you prisoners ...

... you prisoners out there, locked up every day, side by side, with the living ghost of your terrible deeds. Even you in your jail. He sees you there, he sees you and knows what you've done, he knows your sin and he loves you. Jesus loves you.

SELENA. No ...

PREACHER. Jesus died for you. You! I'm talking to you! He put his own body on the cross and died for your sins. Oh, children, oh, children, his own sacred body pierced and bled for your sins. For you. Not the person standing next to you or behind you or across the street from you. No, *you.* I'm talking to you. And I tell you now. Listen to me. I tell you now. No matter what you've done, no matter what crime you have committed, no matter what sin you have embraced, the Lord Jesus Christ will forgive you. He will forgive you. Forgive you. Forgive you. And he will go on loving you.

SELENA. No. I don't think so.

PREACHER. Speak to him from your heart now. Out of your heart, speak to him and receive his love. Oh, Lord ...

SELENA. Oh, Lord ... No, I can't.

PREACHER. Yes. Turn away from the darkness and look into his face, into the eyes of your own savior. Oh, Lord Jesus, my own savior ...

SELENA. Oh, Lord Jesus, my own savior ...

PREACHER. My own savior, who died for my sins ...

SELENA. Who died for my sins ...

PREACHER. Forgive me ...

SELENA. Oh no ...

(SELENA falls to her knees.)

PREACHER. Forgive me ...

SELENA. No. I can't say that.

PREACHER. Go on now. He's listening. After all you've done, you've certainly got his attention.

SELENA. Oh, Lord ...

PREACHER. Let that voice rise up out of your heart ... Speak. Speak.

(Lights fade on PREACHER and isolate SELENA.)

SELENA. *(Very fast.)* Oh, Lord Jesus, my own savior who died for my sins, forgive me. Forgive me. Forgive.

(SELENA remains on her knees.
One female WITNESS enters to play GEORGIA. She looks suspiciously at SELENA. Finally ...)

GEORGIA. Honey, if you're down there waiting for some suckable dick to come along—I can tell you right now, you're at the wrong bus stop. *(No response.)* Hello? Anybody home? Or are we running on empty here? Yo, bitch. I'm talking to you. *(SELENA looks at her.)* That's better. Now, you want to get up off the floor? Or you want a bucket and a mop so you can make yourself look useful?

SELENA. Oh. Georgia?

GEORGIA. Yeah, It's me.

SELENA. I was just listening to the radio.

GEORGIA. And I was just on my way to Elizabeth Arden. That's why I got these roller blades on. Just get up. Get up before you start causing trouble for all of us.

SELENA. I don't think I can get up. I'm stuck.

(GEORGIA offers a hand. SELENA takes it.)

GEORGIA. Your hands are burning up. You got a fever or what?

(GEORGIA feels SELENA's forehead.)

SELENA. It was a gospel station.

GEORGIA. Your head ain't hot.

SELENA. One of those ...

GEORGIA. It's just your hands ...

SELENA. ... religious preacher programs. I guess I got carried away by it.

GEORGIA. I guess you did.

SELENA. He was going on about God and Jesus.

GEORGIA. Yeah. I know. I know. Jesus loves you, so send *me* four dollars.

SELENA. I don't think he was asking for money.

GEORGIA. Ain't nobody talks about God without asking for something. If it ain't your money, it's your soul. And if it ain't your money or your soul—then look out, cause the only other thing they could possibly be after is your pussy.

SELENA. He was talking about something else.

GEORGIA. Uh-huh. Well, let it go.

SELENA. Yes.

GEORGIA. Peddling that shit in here. If they're looking for money, they're broadcasting to the wrong bitches. Ain't they?

SELENA. I heard something. It was so clear. Like a bell going off inside my brain.

GEORGIA. Oh, yeah. I heard that one, too. Bells in the brains. You know what that is? That's every thought you're thinking bouncing off these concrete walls. Making you stranger than you already know you are. Else why else would you be here in the first place? Let it go, bitch. There ain't no help no way coming in here from outside. That's a hope you just got to let die. Otherwise it will kill you. That's what hope is for. To kill you. Hope is the killing thing. You know? I ain't here. I ain't gonna be here long. I shall be released. I ain't really who I am. I ain't really done what I done. Just a great load a shit that you got to get out of your insides. The sooner you flush it down the toilet, the cleaner the air will smell. And you can get on with what little bit of miserable life you got left. Now are you getting up or ain't you?

SELENA. *(Laughs.)* My legs are like pudding ...

GEORGIA. *(Trying to help her up.)* Somebody sees you like this ...

SELENA. ... and my heart is racing away from itself.

(GEORGIA suddenly drops to her knees next to SELENA.)

GEORGIA. Ow! What in hell ...? Now look, sister. You got to get up or let go of me 'cause your hands are getting too hot to hold. What's the matter with you?!

SELENA. I feel ... I don't know. I feel it in my heart. What is it? My stomach, too. Oooh ...

(SELENA puts GEORGIA's hands on her body.)

GEORGIA. Jesus! Jesus Christ Almighty! Let go of me! Let go! Let go!

(SELENA lets go. GEORGIA pulls away. SELENA clutches her belly.
Blood starts to flow from between her legs, staining her dress—bright red. SELENA is more confused than scared.
She touches the wetness, looks at the blood on her hands.)

SELENA. What ... ?
GEORGIA. Selena ... ?
SELENA. What? What did I do? What did I do?

(BLACKOUT. Lights up immediately on GEORGIA.)

GEORGIA. Well, you can believe this or you can disbelieve it, I don't care. Most everybody now don't hardly mention it when they talk about her. That is because they cannot make any kind of sense out of it, no matter which way they try. *(SELENA enters—frail, walking as if on eggs. A soft breeze could knock her down. One WITNESS comes down to SELENA. SELENA holds the WITNESS' hands for a moment. Then slowly, she puts one hand on the WITNESS' shoulder. The WITNESS turns so that SELENA is embracing the WITNESS from behind with one arm around the WITNESS' waist and one hand on the WITNESS' shoulder.)* But the truth is there weren't so sense in it. And unless you're prepared to talk about miracles—which most people ain't—there just ain't a hell of a lot to say about it. Belinda Coyne, she was the first. She had pain in her left shoulder, you would not believe the pain. There was no joint left. Those bones were knit right together, she could not move that arm. Sometimes, at night ...
WITNESS (BELINDA) and GEORGIA. *(Together.)* ... sometimes at night, I (she) roll over in my (her) sleep, roll on top of that shoulder. Oh, God. Oh, God, the pain is like razors...
BELINDA. ... Razors inside cutting their way out.
SELENA. Oh, what a terrible thing.
BELINDA. And they won't give me nothing for it. 'Nothin we can do. You take some aspirin.'

SELENA. You leave it to them, they'd give you aspirin for a flat tire.

(They ALL laugh.)

BELINDA. Yes, they would.

BELINDA and GEORGIA. Oh, yes they would.

SELENA. *(Still holding BELINDA.)* Where is it? Here?

BELINDA. Yes. There it is.

SELENA. Right here?

BELINDA. That heat feels good. What is that?

SELENA. That's just my hand. It gets hot. *(SELENA slides her hand up and down BELINDA's arm.)* Does that feel good?

BELINDA. Yes. But be careful ...

SELENA. I am careful. I am *full* of care.

BELINDA. 'Cause I can't move that arm ...

SELENA. I know that.

BELINDA. I can't even move it but one inch that it don't hurt ...

SELENA. *(Lifting her arm slightly.)* You mean like this?

BELINDA. Yes. Like that.

SELENA. Like this?

BELINDA. This is what hurts.

SELENA. I don't think so.

BELINDA. What are you doing?

(BELINDA's arm starts to rise.)

SELENA. I ain't doing nothing.

BELINDA. Oh, my, you must be doing something.

SELENA. I'm just holding your hand. See? See?

(BELINDA's arm continues to rise. SELENA lets go of the hand. No pain.)

BELINDA. Oh ... oh ... oh ...

GEORGIA. And that arm just floated on up to heaven. And it weren't no hypnosis trance neither ...

BELINDA. ... because to this day, there ain't no pain in that arm. Once it was gone, it was gone. They wanted to do x-rays and such. But I said, no thank you. I said you leave well enough alone. And when they said, but how could this happen—I said well, it must have been the aspirin.

(BELINDA laughs and goes to join the WITNESSES. SELENA and GEORGIA sit down and start playing cards. SELENA's movements are strange, tentative, fragile—like a baby or a very old person. At the same time there is a growing clarity in her eyes and spirit.)

GEORGIA. Well, after that, the bitches was lining up to get themselves touched, to get the 'laying on of the hands,' you know? Everything from the cancer and the H.I.V. all the way down to the headaches, backaches and your ordinary diarrhea.

SELENA. *(Smiles.)* I can't do anything about that.

GEORGIA. You don't know, do you? Not for sure.

SELENA. I guess I don't—not for sure, anyway. But still...

GEORGIA. Yeah. I know. For one thing, you got to figure out, for that one, just where you gonna lay your hands.

(GEORGIA laughs.)

SELENA. Oh, you. I used to have a friend was just like you. She had a mind on her ... just like yours.

GEORGIA. Ain't nobody got a mind like mine.

SELENA. You see? That's just the kind of thing she would say.

GEORGIA. Oh, yeah? Well, that's one bitch I'd like to meet.

SELENA. I can hardly imagine the two of you in the same room. The walls would just explode. And anyway, I lost her. She's gone.

GEORGIA. Was she one of 'yours'?

SELENA. Oh, no, no, no. I lost her in a different way.

GEORGIA. *(Lays down her cards.)* That's gin.

SELENA. Oh, boy. Ten, twenty, five, seven—thirty-two.

*(GEORGIA shuffles and deals. They play again through the
    following.)*

GEORGIA. You ain't thinking straight.

SELENA. No.

GEORGIA. You're tired.

SELENA. It takes it out of me.

GEORGIA. I bet.

SELENA. Like a spigot opens and my insides rush out.

GEORGIA. Every time?

SELENA. Maybe it's more like burning fuel, burning up
the fuel supply. Because of the heat. And because I feel so
cold after.

GEORGIA. You know when you had your hands on Red
Ryan's back, did you know, when you finished, did you know
you went out cold?

SELENA. That's what it is. Going out cold.

GEORGIA. Did you realize?

SELENA. No.

GEORGIA. I didn't think you knew.

SELENA. Going out cold.

GEORGIA. And when you was healing that bitch with the
ovarian cyst and she was screaming bloody murder ...

SELENA. I remember that.

GEORGIA. You was out that time almost three days.

SELENA. Yes. I do remember that.

GEORGIA. So what do you think?

SELENA. About what?

GEORGIA. About how much of this shit you got in you.
About how much it takes to get it out of you. About how much
time you got to go on burning up the fuel supply before you

go out cold for good. I mean, is that a possibility?

SELENA. I don't know.

GEORGIA. Because maybe you should think of saving a little for yourself, you know? Just to keep yourself alive.

SELENA. You don't have to worry about me.

GEORGIA. Well, I know I don't *have* to. But I do. I do worry. Don't you see that?

SELENA. I do now.

GEORGIA. Well, good. You ain't the best looking bitch in this joint. Not by a long shot. And there's plenty others deserve my attention. So when I express my concern and my affection—don't you brush it aside like you're wiping flies off a piece of pie.

SELENA. No. I don't ... I wouldn't.

GEORGIA. I ain't asking for nothing. I never have.

SELENA. I know that. You are my very best friend.

GEORGIA. And I ain't asking for nothing now either. Except that you take enough care of yourself so as to be available in the future for the continuance of these all too exciting Saturday night card games. Gin.

(SELENA reaches across the table and takes the INMATE's hands.)

SELENA. What I believe is this. I believe that I asked for God's forgiveness and he heard me and I believe that this little power in my hands is his answer. I believe that it is his love burning up my body and doing whatever good I can do. And I believe that whatever happens to me in the service of his love is not for me to question. Because the joy that he has put inside my heart is bigger than life itself. And the more I can give of his love, the greater that joy will be.

GEORGIA. Well. I'm glad *one* of us is happy.

SELENA. And you are not?

GEORGIA. Let me say this. There's give and there's take. You know what I'm saying? There's them that give and give and give. And there's them that take, take, take. And them that give, everybody thinks, oh, them's the good people. And them that take, well, they just selfish, *no* good people. But the truth is something entirely different from that. Now you, you're used to the give, give, give. And I ain't making judgments, but the truth is, you got yourself into deep shit with that philosophy. And I would say you are living proof of how wrong a person can go with that way of thinking. And even now— maybe you been blessed and forgiven and whatever else you think happened to you—and now God's love may be shooting out of you like fireworks on the Fourth of July. So you got even more to give and give and give. But I ain't impressed.

Because until you learn to take some, take some of the love that is being offered you—and I ain't just talking about me. I'm talking about all the love that's been coming your way all your life—no matter how strange and sad and small and un- like anything you may have expected—until you face that love and don't run from it or hide from it or kill it—until you learn to take some kind of love from some kind of living human being—well, honey, you can die happy and holy and blessed, but I'm here to tell you, you ain't never really lived.

SELENA. Do you ... do you have love for me?

GEORGIA. Honey, I dream every night about the heat com- ing out of you. I dream about getting my hands on it. Getting my mouth on it. And sucking it down inside me. And then when you go all cold, all tired and used up, whenever you might need it, I dream of putting my lips back on your body and blowing that heat right back into you, right back through your skin and into your heart. I dream of putting the life back into you. I dream of doing that for you. I dream of you letting me do that.

SELENA. Well ...

GEORGIA. Yeah. Well, I must be getting old.

SELENA. Why?

GEORGIA. I never ever had to do *this* much talking to get a bitch into bed before.

(SELENA kisses her hands. GEORGIA kisses SELENA.)

SELENA. She used to put her hands on me. She'd say, what's this? And I'd say, that's my arm. Then she'd say, yes. And what's this? Well, that is my neck. Yes, she'd say, and what are these? *(GEORGIA leaves her as she speaks and goes to join the WITNESSES. During the following, the WITNESSES give GEORGIA a suitcase and an overcoat.)* Well, that's my chest, I'd say. No, she'd say. A chest is something with drawers in it. Well alright, it's my bosom. Bosom is for old ladies, she'd say. Now you tell me what these are because I ain't going to let go of them 'till you say it. Alright I'd say, they are breasts. They are my breasts. And we laughed. She says she'll accept that, but what she really wants to hear is ... And then she'd us one, two, three words that I just couldn't say. I still can't say them. I laugh. And then she grabbed me between my legs and she says, what is this? Huh? What's this? You say what this is. 'Cause I ain't going to let go until you say it. And I said, well then, I ain't never going to say it. Never. Never. Never. *(GEORGIA walks down to SELENA carrying a suitcase and wearing an overcoat.)* And when I was cold, she made me warm Just like she said. And then in January, I was put into the infirmary ...

WITNESS. What happened to you?

SELENA. Oh, it was nothing. It was a flu that turned into pneumonia—she was right. I never did know how to take care of myself.

WITNESS. Did you still have this heat in your hands? This power to heal?

SELENA. Oh, yes. I still had the gift. I have it now.. I just couldn't do anything about myself.

WITNESS. And when you got out of the infirmary ...

SELENA. She was gone. Transferred. And I never got to say good-bye. And I missed my chance to say thank you. *(GEORGIA exits.)* I missed her. I still do. You know, I believe in Angels. I believe that sometimes in your life, you are on a track that is somehow going in the wrong direction. And someone comes along, some human being who sometimes you don't even know, and they cross your path maybe just for an instant. And something is said or something is done or something just happens and in that split second your life is changed. I believe those people are sent to us. I believe they are Angels. I believe she was one of them.

(Lights blaze white. One WITNESS comes down to play the WARDEN.)

WARDEN. Good morning, Selena. How are you today?

SELENA. I am fine, Warden Price.

WARDEN. Looks like we might be getting some rain.

SELENA. Well, that wouldn't be the worst thing to happen.

WARDEN. No. I guess not.

SELENA. How is *Mrs.* Price?

WARDEN. You can call her Eleanor. She'd *like* you to call her Eleanor.

SELENA. Is she feeling any better?

WARDEN. As a matter of fact, yes. I don't know what you did for her.

SELENA. Nothing really ...

WARDEN. I wouldn't say that. Those pains are completely gone.

SELENA. Just an old trick.

WARDEN. She's been tested—I don't know how many times. For ten years, they kept telling her she had stomach ulcers ...

SELENA. No, no ... They're just spasms. I don't know why doctors always want to think the worst—I guess it's just better for business.

WARDEN. I guess so.

SELENA. All she needs to do, whenever she feels that pain coming on, is just sip some hot water ...

WARDEN. After all the money we spent on medication.

SELENA. Just plain hot water.

WARDEN. They even wanted to operate.

SELENA. And the water relaxes the muscles in the esophagus and that's the end of the spasm and that's the end of the pain.

WARDEN. As simple as that.

SELENA. Esophageal spasm—that's what they call it.

WARDEN. I thought at first that you ...

SELENA. Not this time, no. Sometimes all it takes is common sense.

WARDEN. Well.

SELENA. Yes. *(Pause.)* I know about the appeal being denied. If that's what's worrying you.

WARDEN. No. I know you know about that.

SELENA. It's something else then.

WARDEN. In this state, Selena, a person in your situation has a choice of ... well, there are two options. And if the governor does not grant clemency, we have to be prepared, according to the law, to carry out the sentence of the court.

SELENA. Yes. I see.

WARDEN. Now, the choice is of course totally up to you but we do need you to make that decision now.

SELENA. Oh. *(Pause.)* And the choice is between ...

WARDEN. Well, the two options are ...

SELENA. You mean the gas or the lethal injection?

WARDEN. Whichever you ... well, prefer.

SELENA. *(Takes his hand.)* This must be a very difficult conversation for you to have.

WARDEN. I'm sorry.

SELENA. No. No. No. Don't be sorry. It is funny how you go on living every day, bit by bit, forgetting the sentence that hangs over your head. What's the difference?

WARDEN. Beg pardon?

SELENA. Explain to me the difference between these two choices, these two methods.

WARDEN. Well ...

SELENA. Is there a gas chamber?

WARDEN. So to speak.

SELENA. I would be sealed inside.

WARDEN. Yes.

SELENA. Would I be sitting down?

WARDEN. Yes. I don't know if I know all the technical ... Let's see. And then pellets are dropped into a solution of ...

SELENA. Oh, yes. I've seen that.

WARDEN. You have?

SELENA. On television. I saw it in a movie. I don't remember *which* movie. It was some movie star. But they had his face covered. Would they cover my face?

WARDEN. Yes. I believe they would. I believe they do. I believe it's necessary—well, for one thing there are witnesses.

SELENA. People would be watching?

WARDEN. Yes. That's the law.

SELENA. What would I be wearing?

WARDEN. Now, that I don't know. There hasn't been a woman executed in, oh, over twenty-five years. Now the men generally wear the regulations prison uniform. But in your case, for instance, if you choose the lethal injection method, you would be lying down and a dress might not be the best idea.

SELENA. No. But lying down seems like a good idea. Would my face be covered there, too?

WARDEN. Not necessarily. The injection method doesn't produce the same facial contortions that the gas does. So a mask is not necessary. Of course if you preferred a mask, you could certainly have one.

SELENA. No. I don't really like the idea of covering my eyes.

WARDEN. Yes. Then the injection would seem to be the better idea.

SELENA. You know, I didn't really understand before.

WARDEN. Understand what?

SELENA. Well, that I was going to have to die.

(DURING the following, SELENA is dressed and prepared by the WITNESSES according to the process being described. WITNESSES also prepare the stage so that by the end of the description, everything is ready and in place for the execution. A WITNESS plays the PRESS RELATIONS WOMAN.)

P.R. WOMAN. Good evening I am your press representative and I have been instructed to give you ladies and gentlemen of the press the following information. Now, let's see. *(She scans her notes.)* Normally, in preparation for the execution, the condemned person—or the C.P, as I will refer to her from now on—the C.P. is secured to a gurney by wrist and ankle restraints. *(The gurney is brought down. The P.R. WOMAN indicates the wrist and ankle restraints.)*

These restraints—I don't know if you can see—but they are lined with a very soft material to prevent any unnecessary pain. Once the C.P.—the Condemned Person—is secured, then the cardiac monitoring leads and the stethoscope leads are attached. And in each arm, an intravenous injection device is also attached. Next the chaplain will pray with the C.P. And the warden will ask if there are nay last words.

Now, in the case of Ms. Goodall, because she is a woman, particular attention has been given to her special needs. She has been permitted the use of hair curlers and make-up and she will be wearing her own pajamas which are pink and are embroidered around the collar and cuffs with white daisies. The heart monitor leads and the stethoscope will be attached to her breasts in private by the matron. In this case the C.P. will be wearing a bra as well as a diaper—which the matron will attach—also in private. The diaper is necessary because the pancurorium bromide—which is substantially the same poison that certain South American savages us on the tips of their spears—this substance works like a muscle relaxant. And when this muscle relaxant reaches the anal sphincter, there will be a mess.

You should know that this entire process has been re-hearsed—without the C.P. of course. We have made five dry runs and each step has been timed down to the exact minute. There are of course variables. For instance, inserting the needles in the arms of the C.P can be very tricky since ner-vousness tends to make the veins collapse. To avoid any ex-cess pain and/or delay, the warden has included in his execu-tion team two very experienced men who were battlefield corpsmen in Vietnam and who are used to finding veins in all sorts of conditions. Now, as to the execution itself. Once the C.P. is on the gurney, the correctional officers will wheel it into the execution "chamber" ... *(While SELENA is dresing and fixing her hair and make-up, the empty gurney is wheeled into place.)*

... and place it in front of the witness window. Now these are our media witnesses who will report to you in their own words what they saw and heard and felt during the execution. I hope they will be as good as the ones we had for the Bobby Hill execution last October. If you remember how vivid they were— they certainly gave you the sense of being there, didn't they?

Now, once the gurney is in place, the executioners will enter the room from behind the curtain—unseen by the C.P. of course. We use three executioners. Each man takes his posi-tion by one of three large syringes. Each syringe is attached to a line. Now two of these lines will be attached to the C.P. But one line is a "dummy" line. When all three men push their plungers, the muscle relaxant from two of the lines will go into the veins of the C.P. And within seven to eight minutes, the executions will be completed. But the third line will spill harmlessly into this little basket by the gurney. This allows each executioner to think that perhaps he himself did not ex-ecute the C.P. And it allows us—in our own moder way—to carry on the tradition of inserting a blank in the gun of one member of the firing squad.

Well, that's it. The C.P. has not ordered any special meal for this evening. She will be having the regularly scheduled menu for tonight—that is fried chicken livers, collard greens and sheet cake with a peanut butter icing. So ... if there are no questions, we can proceed.

(All the WITNESSES exit the stage. SELENA is ready—monitors attached, I.V. devices attached to her arms, diaper on, pajamas on, make-up on and a few curlers in her hair. She is working on some needlepoint. Next to her on the table are a bible, some paper and a pen. VIVIAN enters.)

VIVIAN. Hello, Selena.

SELENA. Vivian. You did come.

VIVIAN. Yeah. How are you?

SELENA. Well, I had just about given up any kind of hope.

VIVIAN. They said you wanted to see me.

SELENA. I been wanting to see you every day since I been here. But I just didn't have the courage. Finally, I just made myself ask for you. I made it my final request—so I was sure they'd do something about it.

VIVIAN. Well, they did. They sent for me.

SELENA. You look fine.

VIVIAN. Do I?

SELENA. Yes, you do.

VIVIAN. You must need glasses, honey. I'm as far from fine as a girl can get these days.

SELENA. You look fine to me.

VIVIAN. Well, you have a peculiar way of looking at things—I think I can say that now without too many people disagreeing with me.

SELENA. I guess you can.

VIVIAN. I guess I can.

SELENA. Have you been going out? What have you been doing? Who do you see now?

VIVIAN. I work nights at the china factory outlet. I'm on

the register. That's all the people I see. People buying soup
bowls in the middle of the night. We don't talk much. I just
stand there watching them squeeze dimes out of their change
purses. Honest to God, if I could figure out a way, I wouldn't
charge them anything at all. What's this? A paperback bible?

SELENA. (Referring to bible.) I been looking through it
all day, trying to pick and choose what I want spoken at the
funeral. I know the hymns I want. The warden's wife, she's
been coming in to see me every day—she brought me the bible.
She brings in this little portable organ when she comes, too—
it's just this big and it runs on batteries. And she plays that
little thing and we sing! What a noise we make. So I know the
hymns I want. "His Eye Is On The Sparrow." I like that one.
And Mrs. Price, she likes "Hideth My Sout." Remember how
we used to sing that one?

VIVIAN. Last time we sang a hymn together was at my
brother's funeral.

SELENA. Yes. I suppose that's right.

VIVIAN. We were holding hands, comforting each other,
crying our eyes out with the pain of the loss, bereft because
the man we both loved had been taken from us.

SELENA. That's right, too.

VIVIAN. And now you're sitting here cold as a cold fish
talking about yur own funeral as if you expect me to be somehow interested at all in what the hell hymns are going to be
sung or what words from the bible are going to be prayed over
your bones—as if you expect me to care.

SELENA. Ashes.

VIVIAN. What?

SELENA. They cremate you here. There won't be any
bones. Just ashes.

VIVIAN. Well, fine. Just fine.

SELENA. And I guess it ain't so important what they say...

VIVIAN. Not to me it ain't. What do you want from me,
Selena?

SELENA. I want to give you something.

VIVIAN. What? What something?

(SELENA takes out a piece of paper.)

SELENA. First, I want to hold your hands. I want to lay my hands on you.

VIVIAN. Oh, that's right. You been performing little miracles with those hands.

SELENA. I've been able to give some strength to the body and the soul, I think.

VIVIAN. I don't need any strengthening today, thank you.

SELENA. People feel better. If nothing else, they always feel better.

VIVIAN. I feel fine as I am. What else?

SELENA. Alright then. Then I wanted to show you this. (She gives paper to VIVIAN.) That's a statement—they asked me to make a statement. So I wrote this out. It's for the newspapers. But it is really for you.

VIVIAN. What is it? What's it say?

SELENA. It just says that I am sorry. I am, Viv. I am sorry for what I have done. And I am sorry for hte pain that I have caused you and all the others.

VIVIAN. Well ...

SELENA. I know that doesn't make anything any better...

VIVIAN. No. It just makes it worse. Don't it?

SELENA. Why?

VIVIA. You just make it harder for me to hate you. Don't you? And if I do hate you, then all of a sudden I'm the one who's doing something wrong or feeling something wrong and for what I'm feeling, you make me a bad person.

SELENA. No. No, I don't. It ain't wrong, what o feel. It isn't. What you feel is what you feel. Don't ever deny that or judge that or try to hide that. It's taken me six years now in this prison to see who I am. To see how I spent a lifetime fighting the devil and all the badness I thought was inside me, trying to hide it, and the hiding led to the lies and the lies led to—oh, God.

You are only human. That's what I learned here. Day by day, all the separate parts of my life coming together—parts that did not even know each other. And I see now what I had never known—that it was never meant to be a struggle one against the other. It is all the same. It is all one. In every hope some despair, in every love, some kind of hate. And for all the goodness ...

VIVIAN. Don't you preach to me.

SELENA. I'm sorry.

VIVIAN. Don't you dare.

SELENA. No.

VIVIAN. You lied to me.

SELENA. Yes. I did.

VIVIAN. Every day in some way, you lied.

SELENA. Yes.

VIVIAN. You betrayed me.

SELENA. Yes.

VIVIAN. Behind my back, doing one thing. And to my face, something else.

SELENA. Yes.

VIVIAN. You hurt my brother. You made him suffer.

SELENA. Yes, I did.

VIVIAN. Day after day, feeding him poison. Poison.

SELENA. Yes.

VIVIAN. He was a strong man. A good man. And you cut him down. You ripped the life out of him—he was bleeding inside while you prayed and kissed him and covered him with sweetness and light and more lies. Every word, every motion of your hand, every day of your life—a living, breathing killing lie.

SELENA. Yes.

VIVIAN. *(Losing all control.)* Well, I want you to suffer the way he did. The way every one of them did. I want you to be hurt and confused and fall down in agony. I want to watch while you spit blood from your mouth, while you scream in pain. I want to stand over you with the antidote in my hand, with the power to make you stop hurting—only I won't use it. I will stand over you for days—years—as long as it takes. I will listen to you scream and wail in agony and I will not lift a finger to help you. No. I will take what hurts you and I will stretch it out to hurt more slowly and more deeply. I will see you die and it will make my soul feed good. Good. It will make my heart sing. *(She starts to sing a hymn. She breaks down. The hate is spent. She starts to moan.)* Oh. Ohhh. Ohhh.

(SELENA goes to her. VIVIAN pushes her away.)

SELENA. Alright, then. Alright.

(The WARDEN enters.)

WARDEN. I'm sorry, Selena. Miss Baines will have to go now.

SELENA. Alright. That's alright. *(She gets her needlepoint and gives it to VIVIAN.)* Will you take this for me? I don't know why I didn't finish it. I certainly had the time. *(VIVIAN takes it.)* I know that I am not the person that you want to hear say this—But I love you, Viv. I see the hurt and the terrible aloneness inside you and my arms are open to you. To wrap you up in a little comfort—a little comfort at the cold end of the day. You see? I remember. And you remember, too. There was a body that loved you. You remember that. *(She opens her arms. VIVIAN does not go to her. SELENA waits, arms outstretched. VIVIAN turns away.)* You know, that death chamber is my gateway to heaven. I expect to pass over to the biggest, warmest pair of arms ...

(VIVIAN walks downstage. The WITNESSES enter. SELENA goes to the gurney. She lies down on it. The last connections are made to the apparatus.
The WITNESSES take their places to witness the execution.
VIVIAN is downstage, away from the others.)

VIVIAN. The witnesses were all together in a very small room.

WITNESS. Eight feet by thirteen feet.

WITNESS. That was all it was.

WITNESS. There was a guard in there with us.

VIVIAN. He kept rattling coins in his pocket. I remember that. And then they brought Selena in.

WITNESS. They put her right in front of the window.

WITNESS. I don't think she could see us.

SELENA. I see you ... Esther ... John ...

WITNESS. Maybe she could.

SELENA. I see all of you.

WITNESS. She was looking right at us.

SELENA. ... do you carry shoelaces?

VIVIAN. What else? There was a fly in there ...

SELENA. Yes.

VIVIAN. ... buzzing right around her face. Wouldn't you know it? And then, well, I guess it started. They started giving her the injection.

SELENA. ... and the man gets out of his car and goes up to the farmer. Is that right?

WITNESS. She just lay there.

SELENA. ... maybe if it's just a dress ...

WITNESS. Her lips were moving.

SELENA. Not a full length gown.

WITNESS. Praying. I think she was praying.

SELENA. Oh, John, I'm so tired. Is that ... ? Is that ... ?

WITNESS. Or singing.

VIVIAN. The warden was holding up the words to some hymn so she could see them. So maybe she was singing.

SELENA. And the choice is bit by bit forgetting the sentence especially the internal organs and one of them no matter how hard all the parts coming together ... coming together ...

VIVIAN. I don't know what was going on in her mind. *(SELENA starts to hum and occasionally sing a line of the hymn.)* Then after about six minutes—oh, it seemed like a long time. And it was hard to pay attention. I kept thinking about other things. I had to keep reminding myself—well, what was happening. After about six or seven minutes, you could see the color draining out of her face ... *(Lights start to fade.)* It started going from her forehead first. She started going all gray. Her face and then her neck and her ears. And then her hand slipped right out of the strap and she raised her arm in the air as if she were waving—or reaching for something. And then I guess that was it. There really wasn't much to it at all. I wish now that I had let her touch me, hold my hands. It might have made a difference. It certainly would have done no harm. Life is so disappointing. You have to grab what comfort you can. You know? *(VIVIAN looks at the needle point. SELENA starts to hum, singing softly.)* I'll finish this for her. I guess. It has a quote from the Bible on it.

"And Christ said unto her, whoever believes in me and dies, shall live. And whoever believes in me and lives, shall not die. Do you believe me?"

Well, it's something to think about, isn't it?

(VIVIAN walks upstage and joins the other WITNESSES. SELENA continues singing.)

SELENA. *(Singing.)* 'I once was lost, but now I'm found...' *(As she sings, SELENA raises her arm into the air—waving or reaching ...)* '...was blind by now I see ...'

(Lights fade to black.)

END OF PLAY

PROPERTY LIST

<u>ACT I</u>
1 wheelchair (with bag attached to back)
kitchen table with three (3) chairs
6 metal folding chairs
card table
cross stitch sampler with thread, needle and hoop (see script
        for text)
pills in pill bottle
T.V. remote control
lap blanket
bowl with apple sauce and spoon
paper bag with groceries:
        Snickers bar
        1 roll of toilet paper
        Cheese Doodles
        catfood (consumed)
        1 pint of milk
        1 box of rat poison (consumed)
large votive candle (with lighter or matches)
3 plates with remains of dinner
3 napkins
3 glasses
candle in a holder
cigarettes and a lighter
pills in a pill bottle
3 bridal magazines
4 prescription bottles with pills and labels
empty prescription bottles
coffee mug with spoon
small corsage
ambulance gurney dressed as a bed; pillows, sheets, and
        a blanket
folder with letters of recommendation

pram with Baby Doll
baby bottle with formula

<u>ACT II</u>
vial with rat poison
hospital gurney with straps
syringe
microphone for reporter
add 7th folding chair
briefcase with files
legal notepad
pen
blood packet
deck of playing cards
small suitcase
small bible
notepad and pen
folding hospital screen
heart monitor on a cart with small metal bucket
execution gurney with a pad and arm extensions
letter

SUGGESTED COSTUMES

SELENA–ACT I
Pajamas w/white daisies embroidered around neck and cuffs
      slippers
   cat food scene
add: robe
   fortune teller scene
add: slip, dress, shoes, purse
   date with Vivian and John
add: cardigan sweater
   stoned, watching T.V.
remove all layers, wear slip only
   talking to Vivian
add: new dress, same shoes
   wedding scene
add: tailored jacket with corsage on lapel
   with Mrs. Fennell
same, remove corsage from lapel

SELENA—ACT II
   Vivian finds her out
utilitarian dress, cardigan sweater, neckscarf, purse, shoes
   under arrest
remove: sweater, neckscarf
   in prison
same dress, blood pack is preset in dress pocket
   change
denim jeans, prison issued shirt, same shoes
   execution
return to top of ACT I

ESTHER/WITNESS—ACT I
   as young Esther and witness
modest dress w/lace collar and cuffs, crucifix, watch,
      wedding band, comfort shoes

as old Esther
add: sweater, thick, distorting glasses

ESTHER/BELINDA/WITNESS—ACT II
courtroom
add: tailored jacket, neckscarf
    Belinda
simple shapeless dress, cardigan sweater, comfort shoes
    execution
back to young Esther in Act I

VIVIAN/WITNESS—ACT I
cat food scene
pants, dressy t-shirt, jacket, purse, comfort shoes
    with John and Selena
skirt, long turtleneck sweater, shoes
    wedding
full cut slacks, long sweater, earrings and beads,
        bracelets, heels

PROSECUTOR/WITNESS
as prosecutor
2 pc navy suit w/skirt, blouse, heels, pocket square
    execution
bluejeans, old t-shirt, old jacket, old sneakers

JOHN/WITNESS—ACT I
witness and date with Selena
Dickies workpants, lt. blue workshirt, belt, t-shirt, workboots
    finds Selena sick
add: workjacket
    Selena's speech "I saw right away"
remove: jacket, shirt, boots.

JOHN/PREACHER/WITNESS—ACT II
witness and dead John
3 pc. conservative suit, dress shirt, belt, dark shoes, watch
and chain, tie, tie pin, cufflinks
Preacher
remove jacket, roll up shirtsleeves
Witness
back to top of Act II

FORTUNE TELLER/WITNESS—ACT I
wrapskirt, tanktop, hooded sweatshirt, sandals, big earrings

NEWSCASTER
tailored dress, pumps, pearls

GEORGIA/WITNESS—ACT II
denim jeans, white/blue t-shirt, sweatshirt, sneakers,
denim jacket
execution
back to Fortune Teller, top of show

WITNESS/PHARMACIST/JUDGE/WARDEN
as witness
sportjacket, trousers, striped dress shirt, tie, tie bar,
watch, brown shoes
as Judge—Act II
2 pc. suit, dress shirt, tie, judge robe, glasses, shoes
as Warden–execution
remove judge robe
execution
same as top as Act II

WITNESS/WIFE/PHARMACIST/MRS. FENNELL/ PR WOMAN

as witness/wife

old summer dress, shoes, purse, add jacket for witness

as Mrs. Fennell Act I

simple sweatsuit, sneakers

as Mrs. Fennell Act II

dress/sweater combination, shoes, necklace

as PR woman

short skirt, blouse, hose, heels

execution

same as top of show

WITNESS/MAN/PHARMACIST/LAWYER/ NEWSCASTER

as witness/Man

bluejeans, t-shirt, shirt, belt, boots

as lawyer

2 pc. dark suit, dress shirt, tie, shoes

as newscaster

same

execution

same as top of show

Pultizer Prize Winning Plays

ALL THE WAY HOME
James Agee

BOTH YOUR HOUSES
Maxwell Anderson

CRAIG'S WIFE
George Kelly

A DELICATE BALANCE
Edward Albee

FENCES
August Wilson

THE GIN GAME
D.L. Coburn

GLENGARY GLEN ROSS
David Mamet

HELL BENT FOR HEAVEN
Hatcher Hughes

IN ABRAHAM'S BOSOM
Paul Green

From the Samuel French Catalogue

J.B.
Archibald MacLeish

LOOK HOMEWARD, ANGEL
Thomas Wolfe

LOST IN YONKERS
Neil Simon

MEN IN WHITE
Sidney Kingsley

NO PLACE TO BE SOMEBODY
Charles Gordone

OF THEE I SING
Book by
George S. Kaufman and Morrie Ryskind

Music by
George Gershwin

Lyrics by
Ira Gershwin

THE OLD MAID
Zoe Atkins and Edith Wharton

Continued on next page

Pultizer Prize Winning Plays

OUR TOWN
Thornton Wilder

THE PIANO LESSON
August Wilson

THE SHADOW BOX
Michael Christofer

THE SKIN OF OUR TEETH
Thornton Wilder

A SOLDIER'S PLAY
Charles Fuller

STREET SCENE
Elmer Rice

THE SUBJECT WAS ROSES
Frank Gilroy

THEY KNEW WHAT THEY WANTED
Sidney Howard

THE TIME OF YOUR LIFE
William Saroyan